Earth-Friendly Crafts for Kids

Earth-Friendly Crafts for Kids

50
Awesome Things to Make with Recycled Stuff

Heather Smith with Joe Rhatigan

LARK BOOKS
A Division of Sterling Publishing Co., Inc.
New York

Art Director: **Kathleen Holmes**
Photographer: **Evan Bracken**
Cover Designer: **Barbara Zaretsky**
Illustrator: **Orrin Lundgren**
Production Assistance: **Shannon Yokeley**
Editorial Assistance: **Delores Gosnell, Rosemary Kast, Rain Newcomb**

To Hope, whose faith
in people and ability
to find beauty and
value in common
things will inspire
me always.
–H.S.

Library of Congress Cataloging-in-Publication Data

Smith, Heather, 1974-
    Earth friendly crafts for kids : 50 awesome things to make with recycled stuff /
Heather Smith with Joe Rhatigan.— 1st ed.
        p.   cm.
    Includes index.
    Summary: Provides instructions for using recycled materials to create fifty different
crafts and offers tips for an earth-friendly lifestyle.
    ISBN 1-57990340-1
    1. Handicraft—Juvenile literature.   2. Recycling (Waste, etc.)—Juvenile literature.
[1. Handicraft.   2. Recycling (Waste, etc.)]   I. Rhatigan, Joe.   II. Title.

TT160 .S56 2002
745.5—dc21

2002016235

10 9 8 7 6 5 4 3 2 1

First Edition

Published by Lark Books, a division of
Sterling Publishing Co., Inc.
387 Park Avenue South, New York, N.Y. 10016

© 2002, Lark Books

Distributed in Canada by Sterling Publishing,
c/o Canadian Manda Group, One Atlantic Ave., Suite 105
Toronto, Ontario, Canada M6K 3E7

Distributed in the U.K. by Guild of Master Craftsman Publications Ltd., Castle Place,
166 High Street, Lewes, East Sussex, England BN7 1XU
Tel: (+ 44) 1273 477374, Fax: (+ 44) 1273 478606, Email: pubs@thegmcgroup.com,
Web: www.gmcpublications.com

Distributed in Australia by Capricorn Link (Australia) Pty Ltd.,
P.O. Box 704, Windsor, NSW 2756 Australia

If you have questions or comments about this book, please contact:
Lark Books
67 Broadway
Asheville, NC 28801
(828) 253-0467

Manufactured in China

ISBN: 1-57990-340-1

Contents

Introduction	6
Before You Start	8
Earth-Friendly Lingo	11
Plastic Fantastic	12
Metal Madness	44
Paper Works	72
Glass Goodies	110
It Doesn't End Here	140
Templates	141
A Big List of Thanks	142
Index	144

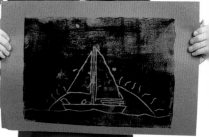

Introduction

What is "Earth friendly"? This is not a book about talking to trees and rescuing baby birds, though we encourage both of those things. Earth friendly means looking at how we use the Earth's resources, how we treat the environment that surrounds us, and coming up with better, safer, cleaner ways of living on Earth. After all, the Earth is really just one gigantic, spinning house we share with countless

plants, animals, and other houseguests. Unfortunately for them, we've taken it over for ourselves and we keep trashing the place.

In this book, you'll find some simple solutions that you can put into action each day to clean up the Earth. The projects and activities on the following pages show you cool ways to reduce, reuse, and recycle the things that we use regularly.

Transform metal cans, tins, and foil into sensational snakes, a lamp, travel games, and musical instruments. Reclaim compact disks, film canisters, and plastic bags to make decorations for your room and yourself. We'll give you ideas for things to make from the odds

and ends in your pockets and junk drawers.
And while you're waiting for the glue to dry
between steps, you'll find fun factoids and
tips to read, think about, remind your parents of. Use them to convince your classmates
to become Earth friendly today!

Congratulations! You're already more aware of
the environmental problems that face the
world's plant, animal, and human life than any
generation before you, thanks in part to computers,
the World Wide Web, and television. And the
fact that you're reading this right now means
that you care about how your life and how
the world around you will take
shape in the 21st century. With
curious, smart people like you out
there, we're bound to find some
better ways of doing things and

living together. You can't run off to save a forest
tomorrow (though it would be a great excuse for
being late to math class), but you can make a
difference by being Earth friendly at home, at
school, and in your community, every day. It starts
with those three Rs you're more than familiar
with: reduce, reuse, recycle. The
less new stuff we make, the less
we take from the Earth's cupboard of natural resources and
each other. The more things
that we reuse and recycle, the
cleaner our Earth will
get, providing
everyone on it
with a healthier
and happier home.

BEFORE YOU START

Avoid future headaches by doing a little preparation before jumping into the projects in this book. You'll save time and make less mistakes by gathering all the tools you need, setting up your work space, and figuring out how to clean up before you cut that first piece of cardboard or start squeezing the glue.

Work Space

Successful artists and crafters have studios, so set up a space in your room or in your house where you can work on your projects. Choose an area that has a table or large floor space to work on, and protect the surface by covering it with newspapers or a large sheet. You'll likely need a window for ventilation and an electrical outlet nearby. If you have pets or younger siblings, be certain they won't be able to get into your crafting tools and materials when you're not watching. The ideal work space allows you to leave your projects and materials overnight without anyone or anything getting into them.

Measuring

If you want your projects to look awesome, start by using a pencil and ruler to make even cuts and neat designs. A compass is handy for making circles, but you can also use a bowl or jar lid as a guide.

Using the Templates

On page 141, you'll find patterns, called *templates*, for some of the projects in this book. Enlarge or reduce the template you need on a photocopy machine to fit the size of your project. You may also trace over the designs with white paper and a pencil. Cut the templates from the paper and tape them in place on your project to use them as stencils for your design. If you have a computer and scanner at home, you can scan the templates and enlarge or reduce them before printing them.

Cutting

A heavy-duty pair of scissors is all you'll need for most of the projects in this book. When working with aluminum cans, you'll need a pair of wire cutters or nail clippers to cut through the rims. On occasion, you may want to use a craft knife; it's a helpful tool for cutting designs and circles from cardboard.

USING A CRAFT KNIFE

Before using a craft knife, set the item you want to cut on top of a scrap piece of wood or thick cardboard to protect the surface below. Hold the craft knife firmly in one hand and press the tip of the knife into the material you're cutting. Slowly drag the knife toward you to make a cut. Never leave craft knives out where pets or young kids might find them.

Sticky Stuff

For temporary attachments, use tape. Duct tape and packing tape are strong and ideal for projects such as the Newspaper Shelf on page 104. The standard white craft glue you've been using since kindergarten will also stick most of the projects in this book together. It dries clear and holds paper, fabric, cardboard, and small pieces of plastic, metal, and glass together. It's also called PVA glue and usually says "nontoxic" on the label. Rubber cement is perfect for sticking paper or fabric to paper and cardboard. Make sure you open a window before using rubber cement, the smell is awful and can make you sick. Washable glue is helpful if you tend to get glue all over the place, because you can use a damp rag to wash smudges off your project. Silicone adhesive is great for projects, such as the Luau Snow Globe

on page 112, where the glued part of the project will get wet. Epoxy comes in all different formulas, and you just need to check the label to find the one that will fit your project. We use it to stick odd-shaped metal or plastic objects together.

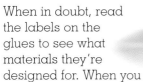

When in doubt, read the labels on the glues to see what materials they're designed for. When you need to cover a large area with glue, use a paintbrush or sponge to spread the glue evenly onto the material. Keep all glues out of the reach of pets and young kids, and make sure you get plenty of fresh air while using them.

HOT GLUE GUN AND GLUE STICKS

Hot glue from a glue gun allows you to attach materials that wouldn't stick together using other glues. You can get clear or colored glue sticks to use with a glue gun, and some even have glitter mixed into them to add sparkle to your design. Once you plug in the glue gun, it heats the glue stick to a hot liquid that oozes out when you squeeze the trigger. Put the tip of the glue gun on the object you want to stick something to and squeeze a line of glue along its surface. Press the piece you want to stick to the object and hold it in place for a few seconds. The hot glue cools and hardens quickly to hold your pieces in place, which is especially helpful if you're decorating odd-shaped items. Rest the glue gun in a stand or on a plate while in use. Remember to unplug the glue gun when you're finished with it and also any time you leave your work space. If you don't want to use a glue gun, experiment with other glues to see what works best.

DECOUPAGE GLUE

Decoupage is what you do when you make a collage or design by cutting and pasting layers of paper or fabric to cover the surface of an object. An example, is the Salvaged Seat on page 98. To make your own decoupage glue, mix four parts white craft glue to one part water in a glass jar. Cover it with a lid so it'll be ready to use for your collages and decoupage projects. This watered-down glue mixture also makes a great protective coating over paper and fabric projects.

Painting

We recommend acrylic craft paints throughout this book because they dry quickly and can be used to cover almost any surface. Use sandpaper to rough up metal surfaces so that paint will stick to them better, and mix in a little glue with your paint for plastic objects. You can buy specialty glass paints and fake lead line strips to transform plain glass jars and mirrors to look like stained glass. Glow-in-the-dark paints and three-dimensional (3-D) paints are great for special effects. If you use spray paint, make sure you work outdoors so you get plenty of fresh air. Protect your hard work by coating the surface with clear nailpolish, a water-based sealer, acrylic spray enamel, or a couple of coats of decoupage glue.

Paintbrushes come in all sorts of sizes, shapes, and textures. Foam brushes and old sponges spread paint evenly over most surfaces and are easy to clean. Keep a variety of paintbrushes and sponges, a jar of water, and a rag within reach for successful paint jobs.

Extras

You can also decorate your projects with colorful wire, string, beads, glitter, and odds and ends from a kitchen junk drawer to make them unique.

Helpful Stuff

You may have never used some of the tools in this book before, but we recommend them to save you time and effort when making your projects.

Use a hammer and nail or a drill when you need to make holes in wood, metal, or plastic. Always place a block of wood under the object you're hammering or drilling to protect your work surface. You'll need a tumbler to smooth the edges around the pottery shards for decorating the Better-Than-A-Broken-Dish-Tray on page 117.

Tumblers are sold at most craft stores and are also used to polish rocks. If you're not familiar with how to use a hammer, drill, or tumbler, please don't attempt to figure them out on your own. Which brings us to...adults. They're really great to have around when you can't figure out what to do, you need an extra hand, or crave a snack to fuel your imagination. And we bet you'll have more trouble keeping adult hands out of your work space once they see the cool things you're making. We've provided a whole range of projects in this book, from easy to challenging, so for your safety and fun, look for "Adult Assistance Necessary" on projects that require an adult's help.

Cleaning Up

Recycle all your metal, paper, and plastic scraps, or keep them in an old suitcase or box for future projects. Store excess glue or paint in glass jars with lids. Acrylic paints and water-based glues can be cleaned up with warm, soapy water. Dispose of empty paint and glue containers in a safe and eco-minded way. (Don't just drop them in the garbage can.) Read the labels for safe disposal tips, or call your city's sanitation department for advice. Some communities have special programs for collecting and reusing certain types of paint, and facilities that specially process chemical materials. Don't be hasty or careless about cleaning up your craft materials. Plan how and when you'll clean up before you start any project.

Finally ...

Use your common sense, and ask for help when you need it. And whatever you do, have fun. Okay, we're done here.

Earth-Friendly Lingo

Here's your guide to the Earth-friendly terms you'll see throughout this book, in the news, and on the Internet. So if you're wondering what the difference is between "reuse" and "recycle" or what "sustainable" means, read on.

Acid rain. Rainwater is naturally a little acidic, but when chemicals in the atmosphere (mostly sulfur dioxide and nitrogen dioxide from burning coal and automobile exhaust) mix with water vapor, the resulting rainwater can turn as acidic as vinegar. Acid rain, snow, or fog harms plants, affects soil and water quality, and damages man-made buildings and stonework.

Biodegradable. A substance that can be naturally broken down into harmless elements by bacteria and other organisms.

Biodiversity. The number and variety of living things in a particular ecosystem. Also, the number and variety of living things and ecosystems on earth.

Conservation. The protection, restoration, and management of wildlife, natural resources, or ecosystems.

Ecosystem. All of the living and nonliving things plus their interactions that create and define a particular place.

Ecology. The study of how living things interact with each other and with the nonliving things that surround them.

Endangered species. A plant, animal, or other living thing whose population has decreased so much that it may become extinct.

Environment. Everything that surrounds a living creature and affects it.

Extinct. When a particular type of plant, animal, or other living species no longer exists on Earth.

Fossil fuels. Coal, oil, natural gas and other substances that formed from plant and animal remains deep in the earth's crust. These carbon-rich substances release energy and carbon dioxide when burned.

Global warming. The Earth's atmosphere acts like a greenhouse, trapping gases and heat around the Earth. Carbon dioxide gas released from burning fossil fuels is building up in the atmosphere and heating up the Earth at a rate higher than scientists believe is natural. If temperatures continue to increase as they have since the 1980s, scientists predict the polar icecaps will melt, weather patterns will change, and the seas will rise.

Habitat. The place where an animal, plant, or other living thing finds food, shelter, water, and room to grow.

Hazardous waste. Trash that is harmful to humans or the environment, especially if it is likely to catch fire, explode, release toxins, burn skin, or corrode metals.

Incinerator. A facility that burns trash, sometimes for energy.

Landfill. A designated pit or hole dug into the ground where collected trash is dumped. In a sanitary landfill, each new layer of trash is covered with dirt, and the bottom of the pit is lined to help prevent groundwater contamination.

Litter. Trash that has been carelessly tossed out instead of being recycled or disposed of properly.

Nonrenewable resource. Something that has a limited supply or takes thousands of years to regenerate, such as fossil fuels, topsoil, and precious metals.

Pollution. Substances added to the air, water, or soil that are unnatural and can harm living things or cause undesirable changes in the environment.

Recycle. To collect unwanted materials and process them to make new materials that can be used again.

Reduce. To limit the amount of stuff you throw away by purchasing items you can use more than once, making your own stuff, and choosing goods that have minimal packaging.

Renewable resource. Things such as trees, solar energy, wind, and water, which naturally regenerate after they're used or have an endless supply.

Reuse. To take something old and fix it up or find a new way to use it.

Sustainable. Methods that protect and provide for future generations of living things and the environment.

PLASTIC
fantastic

There are dinosaurs in your plastic wrap.

There are dinosaurs in your computer monitor.

And, yes, there are even dinosaurs in
your CD collection.

Of course you can't see them; they've been dead for millions
of years. But it's from their carbon-rich remains that
we've struck oil. And oil is what we humans use to make

plastic. Take a look around
your room and in your
trash can. There's a whole
lot of plastic in there,
isn't there?

Plastics have made our
lives easier and lighter. A
plastic jug full of milk is
heavy, but imagine if it
were made of glass. Yikes!
Dropping it would really
be a disaster. Goods
packed in plastic save

space and are lightweight and convenient, but all that
disposable packaging is filling up our landfills and litter-
ing the planet. Maybe you're fortunate to live where you
can recycle most of the plastic you discard, but in many
parts of the world that option doesn't exist, and plastic
litter is taking over. Loose plastic not only looks trashy
but is also life-threatening for animals that eat it or
get tangled in it.

Fortunately, creative people have invented amazing ways to recycle and reuse plastic. Fleece, spun from recycled plastic fibers, is comparable to sheep wool when it comes to warmth and comfort in outdoor clothing. Recycled plastic lumber is strong and long-lasting and is showing up in park benches and playgrounds all over. As you read this, chemists and engineers are developing new forms of plastic made from vegetable oils that will naturally and harmlessly break down over time.

So what are you waiting for? Dive into that trash can and salvage all of that plastic to make fantastic new creations. Save your film canisters, container lids, grocery bags, and compact disks to make glow-in-the-dark mobiles, disco balls, sensational snakes, fabulous jewelry, and so much more.

SENSATIONAL SNAKES

In many cultures, snakes are a symbol of rebirth because they shed their skin. These snakes represent the possibilities of new uses for all the things we throw away every day. Collect all those caps and lids you can't recycle, and string them together for your own sensational snake.

What You Need

Lots of jar lids (plastic and metal) and bottlecaps*

Scrap piece of wood to work on

Hammer and nail

Drill with $1/8$-inch (3 mm) bit (optional)

Aluminum foil, foam football, tennis ball, or plastic bottle

Bottlecaps, marbles, beads, or golf balls

Acrylic paints or markers (optional)

Scissor

$1/8$-inch-diameter (3 mm) plastic-coated wire

Needle-nose pliers

Hot glue gun and glue sticks or silicone adhesive

* Ask the staff at your school cafeteria if they'll collect caps for you.

What You Do

1. Set one lid on the scrap piece of wood with the inside of the lid facing up. Punch a hole in the lid's center with the hammer and nail. If there's an adult nearby, you can use a drill to make the hole more quickly. Repeat with the rest of the lids and bottlecaps.

2. Sort all of the lids and bottlecaps into piles by color and size.

3. Look for items that are shaped like a snake's head and made from materials you can easily make holes in or glue things to. Aluminum foil, foam footballs, tennis balls, and plastic bottles are just some of the things that make great heads. Use small bottlecaps, marbles, beads, golf balls—you get the idea—for eyes. As you collect your materials, keep in mind whether you're going to glue these things together or tie them together with wire or string. You can also use acrylic paint or markers to draw a face.

4. Look at all the piles around you and at the objects you've gathered, and decide what kind of snake you want to make. Take the object you've chosen for the snake's head and decide which side is the front and which side is the back. Cut, drill, or poke a ⅛-inch (3 mm) hole through the head from where the mouth will be to where the head will connect to the body. Ask an adult for help if you need to use a drill or sharp object to make this hole.

what the . . !?

5. Tie a knot 6 inches (15.2 cm) from one end of the wire (to make the tongue) and feed the other end of the wire through the hole in the snake head. Pull the wire tightly to make sure it doesn't slip through the head. If it does, make a bigger knot.

6. Slide the wire through the holes in the lids and bottlecaps, and string them together to make the snake body. Push the caps together toward the head as you add them to the wire. Stop when you're 4 inches (10.2 cm) from the end of the wire.

7. Use the needle-nose pliers to twist the last bit of wire into a tight knot. Your snake now has a tail.

8. There are many ways to attach the eyes to the snake's head. If the eyes are lightweight, use a dab of hot glue on them and press them in place against the head. For heavier eyes, make a hole through the head from one side to the other where you want the eyes to be. Cut a piece of wire to fit through the hole and use the needle-nose pliers to tie one eye to each end of the wire.

Now that you've made your first snake, imagine making one to wrap around your entire school! With your principal's permission, host a snake-making competition between classes or grades. Challenge your classmates to collect as many lids and bottlecaps as possible.

CD Disco Ball

A couple of these disco balls will add some serious sparkle to your next party. Put on some funky music, shine a couple of flashlights at the balls, and dance under a ceiling of spinning stars.

What You Need

Several old compact disks (CDs) *

Heavy-duty scissors

Polystyrene foam ball

Silver metallic spray paint

Hot glue gun and glue sticks

Fishing line or string

Rubbing alcohol or nail polish remover (optional)

Clean rag (optional)

* To start a throwaway CD collection, ask your parents if they have any old CD data files at work that are no longer needed, check your mailbox for junk-mail CDs, or ask friends for their scratched, useless music CDs.

What You Do

1. Cut the CDs into small triangular-shaped pieces with the heavy-duty scissors, and collect the pieces in a container until you have enough to cover the foam ball. If your scissors are sharp and sturdy, cutting the CDs will be no problem. Don't worry if some of the CD pieces crack in places, everybody will be too busy dancing to notice.

2. Find an area outdoors to use the spray paint that is far from objects you don't want to accidently spray. Lay the ball on some newspaper, and paint it with the metallic spray paint. Let it dry, and then bring it back inside.

3. Squeeze hot glue onto a small section of the ball, and press the CD pieces to the ball until the area is covered.

(Make sure the shiny sides of the CD pieces are face up.) Repeat until the entire ball is covered. Try to fit the pieces together like a puzzle to fill in any gaps, but don't worry if there are some small holes between the CD pieces. From a distance, the metallic paint will help hide them.

4. Cut a piece of fishing line as long as your arm, and hold the ends together on one spot on the ball. Use a dab of hot glue on top of the ends to stick them to the ball.

5. Hang the ball from the ceiling in a place where you can direct light at it. Clean the disco ball with a towel soaked in a little rubbing alcohol or nail polish remover for maximum shine.

PACK AN EARTH-FRIENDLY LUNCH

Hold your nose and take a look inside your trash can. If it's like the one in most households, you'll find all kinds of leftover packaging in there. Now think about the trash cans in your school's cafeteria. Yuck! Single-serving containers of your favorite lunch foods are convenient when you're short on time, but most of that cool-looking packaging can't be recycled and ends up in the garbage. Keep those trash cans empty, and save resources by packing an Earth-friendly lunch every school day. Imagine the resources that would be saved if everyone in your school followed your lead.

- Instead of disposable juice boxes and bags, pour your favorite drink into a leak-proof bottle.

- Reuse yogurt, margarine, dip, and hummus containers to hold snacks.

- Declare an end to soggy, squished sandwiches, crumbled cookies, and broken chips by keeping them safe in a solid, resealable container.

- Cloth napkins save forests, and you can use them hundreds of times.

- Don't throw away that perfectly good plastic spoon. Wash it and use it again.

- Pack it all up in a fabric or plastic lunch bag to keep your hot food warm and cold food cool.

Odds & Ends Alert!

Throughout this book you'll find the logo

ODDS & ENDS

next to some projects. This logo means that the project you're about to attempt is way too strange, weird, or wonderful to fit into any one category or chapter. These are projects that prove beyond a reasonable doubt that you can make something out of just about anything, including old bowling balls, ripped jeans, useless crayon pieces, and even a flat bicycle tire. So dig through that scary junk drawer in the kitchen, scrounge through Grandma's attic, and enjoy the Odds & Ends we've scattered throughout this book.

POCKET PEOPLE

These pocket people were born out of all the little things that collect in pockets and junk drawers. Reach into a pocket right now. (Yes, right now...we'll wait.) Discover anything useful? Lint, lollipop sticks, broken pencils, paper clips, buttons, bottlecaps? These useless, random items that you picked up somewhere along the way have suddenly become quite handy, haven't they? The only rule with pocket people is that there are no rules. The possibilities are endless.

What You Need

Old fishing floats*

Screws, springs, bottlecaps, washers, twigs, shells, toothpicks, wire, pens, and anything else that can be turned into a body part

Glue, silicone adhesive, self-adhesive magnet, and/or duct tape

Screwdriver (optional)

Acrylic craft paints and paintbrush (optional)

*The bodies of these pocket people are actually old fishing floats that were found washed up on a beach. But a scrap of wood, block of foam, broken cup, small can, or part of an old toy are some examples of the things that could be used for the base of your figure. You could even make a body out of modeling clay or salt dough, and shape it to look more like a human or animal form.

What You Do

1. Once you've gathered the materials you'd like to use, begin by playing with the pieces until you have a face or body you like.

2. When attaching the body parts to the body, experiment a little with glues and tapes to see what works best. If the body of your pocket person is soft enough, use a screwdriver to poke holes where you want to attach parts. If the body is more solid, use a strong glue or silicone adhesive. You can also cut strips of self-adhesive magnet to stick parts to a metal can.

3. Use the acrylic paints to add any finishing touches you want. Your pocket person is now done and will forever be a symbol of how even the most useless of things can have meaning when a little creativity is put into action.

CD Fashion Statements

"Why dahling, wherever did you get those fabulous jewels?"

"Well dahling, I made them myself. And you can, too, with a few tools, some CDs, and a little bit of imagination. Your set of shimmery CD jewelry is just a few steps away, dahling."

What You Need

Template on page 141 or sketching materials

White paper and pencil

2 to 3 old compact disks (CDs)

Tape

Heavy-duty scissors

Acrylic paint, colors of your choice

Paintbrush

Drill with drill bit as wide as the cord

Leather cord or string

Jump rings*

Needle-nose pliers

Earring posts*

Beads

Hot glue gun and glue sticks or epoxy

Pin back*

Clear nail polish

* Available in the jewelry-making section of craft stores

What You Do

1. Copy the templates on page 141 to a piece of white paper, or sketch some designs of your own. Cut out the jewelry designs and tape them to the backs of the CDs.

2. Cut out the shapes with the scissors. If your scissors are sharp and sturdy, cutting the CDs will be no problem. Trim any sharp points in the cutout designs, so you don't end up poking yourself while wearing the jewelry.

3. Paint two coats of acrylic paint on the written side of the cutout CD shapes. Let them dry.

4. For the necklace, have an adult help drill the holes (as indicated on the templates) in the CD pieces so you can hang them from the cord.

5. Pry open each of the jump rings with the needle-nose pliers. Slide a jump ring through the hole in each CD necklace piece, then press the ring back together with the pliers.

6. Thread the cord through the jump rings and alternate the CD pieces with the beads to make the necklace. Tie the ends of the cord together or around a necklace clasp and check for fit.

7. For the ear-rings, glue the CD pieces to the ear-ring posts. Decorate the earrings with beads or paint.

8. For the pin, glue extra shapes on top of the first CD piece. When the glue dries, glue the design to the pin back.

9. Protect your jewelry by brushing the surface with clear nail polish.

GLOW-IN-THE-DARK MOBILE

Collect some of your parents' or grandparents' old vinyl record albums (those big, black, round things people played before CDs were invented), and turn them into something worth spinning again. With glow-in-the-dark paint you can bring vinyl into the space age. Just make sure you have your parents' permission before you turn their Beatles albums into ceiling art.

What You Need

Old scratched or discarded vinyl records

Compact disks (CDs)

Bottlecaps wider than the holes in the records

Glow-in-the-dark paint, in squeeze bottles

Scrap piece of wood

Hammer and nail

Wire

Needle-nose pliers

What You Do

1. Decorate all the records, CDs, and bottlecaps with the glow-in-the-dark paint (see the project photographs for some ideas). Let them dry.

2. Set the bottlecaps on the scrap piece of wood, with their insides facing up, and make a hole in the center of each one with the hammer and nail.

3. Arrange the records, CDs, and bottlecaps in the order you want them to hang. For this mobile, slide one bottlecap on the wire followed by the record and four more bottlecaps. Alternate CDs and bottlecaps until the mobile is as long as you want it to be.

4. Use the needle-nose pliers to twist the end of the wire under the last bottlecap into a knot to hold the mobile together. Make a loop at the top of the wire to use for hanging the mobile. Charge the glow-in-the-dark paint under a bright light, then turn the lights out to see your artwork shine.

Cap & Lid Curtain Alarm

A low-tech solution to an age-old problem, this simple doorway curtain is guaranteed to alert you when younger brothers or sisters try to sneak in.

What You Need

Tape measure

20-gauge wire or heavy string

Heavy-duty scissors

Lots of lids (plastic and metal) and bottlecaps

Scrap piece of wood

Hammer and nail*

Tape

Beads (optional)

Needle-nose pliers

Sturdy curtain rod

*With help from an adult you could use a drill instead of the hammer and nail.

What You Do

1. Decide where you want to hang your curtain, and measure the length of the doorway (from the top of the door frame to the floor).

If plastic bags take up to 20 years to biodegrade in a landfill, how long does it take other materials we often throw away? Here are the answers!

Paper: 2 months

Orange peel: 5 months

Milk carton: 6 months

Shoe: 40 years

Plastic bottle: 450 years

Aluminum can: 500 years

Fishing line: 600 years

Glass bottle: 1 million years

Polystyrene foam: never—Wow!

Cut five to seven pieces of wire or string (depending on how many strings of lids you want) approximately 6 inches (15.2 cm) longer than the doorway.

2. Set each lid and bottlecap, face-down, on the scrap piece of wood, and punch holes in the centers of each with the hammer and nail.

3. Sort all of the lids and bottlecaps into piles by color and size. Look at all the piles around you and think about the patterns you can make for your curtain. You could make strings of all the same-size lids, or mix them up, as we did for our curtain.

4. Bend the top of one of the wires into the shape of a loop, and use the needle-nose pliers to twist the wire around itself below the loop so it won't slip out. Repeat for the rest of the wires.

5. Slide the caps and lids onto the wires up to the loops. Wrap a piece of tape around the wire under each of the lids and caps to hold them in place. The tape will also keep the lids from falling to the bottom of the wire. You can also use beads in the spaces between the caps.

6. Twist the bottom of the wire into a loop to hold the last cap or lid in place.

7. Slide the top loop of each wire onto the curtain rod and hang the curtain in your doorway.

27

CAP & LID CURTAIN ALARM

Plastic Bag Mat

Keep your plastic bags out of the dump by weaving them into a really cool floor mat that not only takes punishment but also feels quite comfy beneath your feet.

What You Need

Rectangular piece of cardboard, a little bit larger than the mat you want to make

Scissors

Yard or meter stick

Pencil

Wide ribbon

Plastic grocery bags

What You Do

1. The cardboard serves as the loom for weaving your mat. Your finished mat will end up being about 3 inches (7.6 cm) shorter than the cardboard, which is why the cardboard is slightly larger than the mat you plan to make.

2. Create the loom by cutting notches along the top and bottom ends of the cardboard to hold the ribbon you'll wrap around it.

3. Set the cardboard on the floor in front of you so that it's vertical (the long sides run up and down). Use the ruler as a guide to draw a line across the cardboard, 1½ inches (3.8 cm) below the top edge.

Fig. 1

Make a mark, every 1½ inches (3.8 cm) along the line you just drew.

4. At each mark, cut a notch as wide as your thumb from the edge of the cardboard to the line (figure 1).

5. Use the notches as guides for wrapping the ribbon around the front and back of the loom (photo 1). When you've wrapped the ribbon all the way across the cardboard, tie the ends together on one of the sides (photo 2). Your loom is now ready for weaving.

1

2

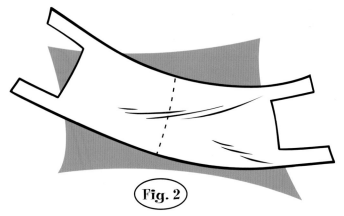

Fig. 2

6. Snip the handles on all of the bags, then cut down the sides of each bag to the bottom seam. Open up each bag so it looks like figure 2.

7. Tie the ends of the bags together to make "yarn" (photo 3).

3

8. Tie one end of the yarn to the ribbon at the top corner of the loom, then weave the rest of the yarn over and under the ribbon, all the way around the loom (photo 4). Weave each row in an opposite pattern from the row above it. For example, in row one, if you weaved the yarn under the first piece of ribbon, over the second piece of ribbon, and so on, then start row two by weaving the yarn over the first piece of ribbon, under the second piece of ribbon, and so forth.

9. Scrunch the rows of yarn toward the top of the loom after finishing each row, so the mat won't have any gaps in it. Continue weaving the yarn around the loom until you reach the bottom. Tie the yarn to the last ribbon on the side of the loom.

10. Cut the ribbon across the top edge of the loom (photo 5). Slide the cardboard out from the center of the mat, then tie the ends of the ribbon together in pairs. Cut the ribbon at the bottom of the mat, and tie the ends in pairs. Kick off your shoes and test out your new mat—you'll be amazed how cushy it feels.

4

5

♻ PLASTIC SCAVENGER HUNT

The plastics identification codes were developed by The Society of the Plastics Industry, Inc. in 1988, and have since been adopted by recyclers and manufacturers worldwide.

Search your house for discarded plastic containers that have these symbols printed on them.	Recycle the old containers so they can be transformed into these new materials.
1 PETE plastic soft drink and water bottles	bottles, fleece, carpet, furniture
2 HDPE milk and juice jugs, liquid detergent bottles, yogurt containers	bottles, drainage pipe, oil containers, lumber, floor tile, recycling bins
3 PVC pipes, bottles, packaging films, synthetic leather products, tubing	plumbing parts, hoses, tile, bottles
4 LDPE garbage bags, black plastic sheeting, bread bags, squeeze bottles, clothing, carpet, furniture	film, compost bins, floor tile, lumber, shipping envelopes
5 PP margarine tubs, screw on tops, medicine bottles, lunch boxes	recycling bins, ice scrapers, bicycle racks, auto battery cases, brushes
6 PS carryout food containers, packing peanuts, coffee cups, meat trays, compact disk cases	foam packing materials, thermometers, insulation, rulers, desk trays
7 OTHER refillable water jugs, some juice containers, nylon, acrylic, and mixtures of plastics	lumber and specially designed products

COMING TO A GROCERY STORE NEAR YOU?

Plastic bags make life a whole lot easier, but the same qualities that make them so great have also gotten them into trouble. Plastic bags were created to last; it takes 20 years for them to naturally break down or biodegrade. According to the United States Environmental Protection Agency, over 200,000 tons (180,000t) of plastic bags are produced each year, and the world uses over three billion bags a year. In parts of South Africa, Japan, and Nepal, plastic bag litter and growing trash heaps have become such problems that stores now charge fees for packing goods in plastic bags. Some communities even forbid stores from using them at all.

STAMPING WITH POLYSTYRENE FOAM

Poly what? Polystyrene foam. You know, the stuff used to make carryout food boxes, coffee cups, and packing trays for meat and produce. It can't be recycled in most communities, so we've come up with a great fun way to keep it out of the trash. The soft material is easy to carve and is perfect for printing and stamping. Use an entire tray as a printing block, or cut a container into smaller pieces to use as stamps.

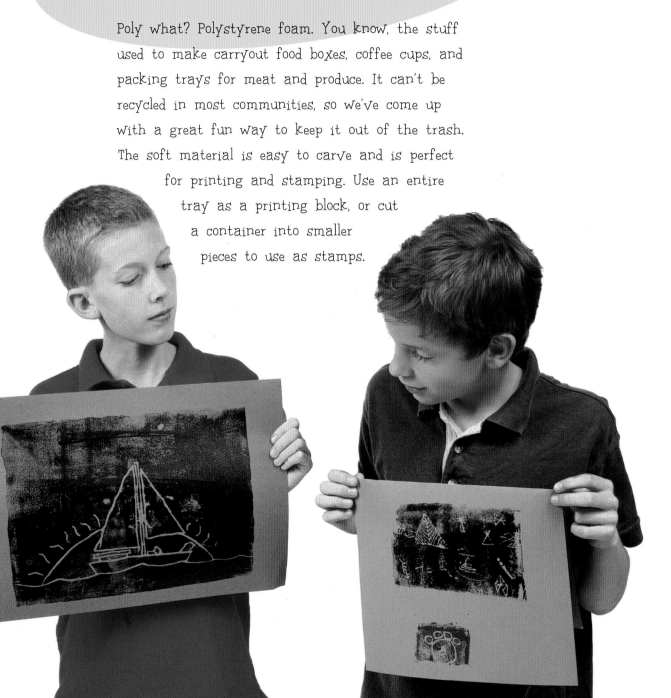

What You Need

- Polystyrene foam tray (for a printing block)
- Marker
- Pencil or pen
- Paint
- Wide paintbrush or brayer
- Paper
- Glass jar
- Polystyrene foam carryout container (for stamps)
- Scissors (for stamps)
- Small square pieces of cardboard (for stamps)
- Glue (for stamps)
- Several bottlecaps (for stamps)

What You Do

1. Clean the tray with hot, soapy water and dry it with a towel.

2. To make a printing block, set the tray upside down on a table. Draw your design on the tray with a marker, then use a pencil or pen to carve the image into the tray (photo 1). The design can be as simple or complicated as you like. Note: If there's a raised imprint or code on the tray, it'll show up in the design.

3. Use the wide paintbrush or brayer (like the one shown below) to spread a thin layer of paint over the design on your tray (photo 2).

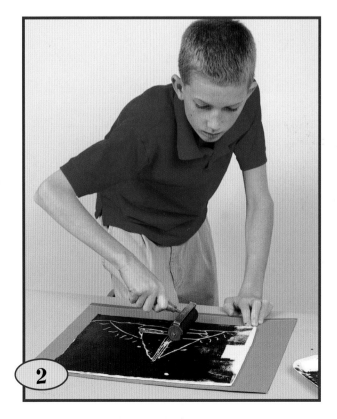

4. Carefully and evenly lay a piece of paper over the design on the tray. Roll the glass jar over the paper, or rub the surface with your hand, to transfer the design (photo 3).

5. Slowly peel back a corner of the paper to see if the printing worked (photo 4). If it looks good, go ahead and peel the rest of the paper off. If the design isn't clear, press the corner of the paper back down and roll the jar over the paper a few more times before lifting the paper again.

6. Make individual stamps by cutting designs from a larger piece of polystyrene, then glue cardboard to the backs of the designs. Make handles for the stamps by gluing bottlecaps, facedown, to the cardboard pieces. Press each stamp into a tray of paint, and stamp it on a scrap piece of paper until the design shows up clearly. You're now ready to stamp away.

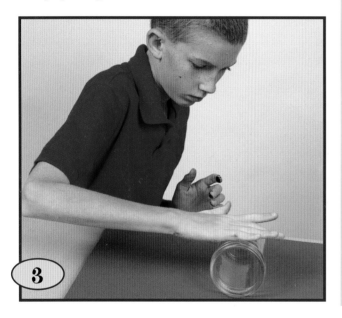

3

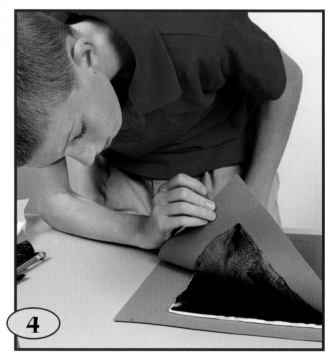

4

FABULOUS FILM CANISTER MINI-LIGHTS

Everybody loves collecting 35mm film canisters; they just look too useful to throw away. But there aren't many folks who actually know what to do with them once they've collected a bunch. Well, this project finally puts these canisters to good use. After decorating your strand of lights, hang them up in a favorite corner of your room or use them to color an otherwise dark closet.

What You Need

A strand of mini-lights (for indoor use)

White or clear plastic film canisters

Drill with assorted bits

Several sheets of colored tissue paper

Pencil

Scissors

Ruler

Decoupage glue (see page 9)

1/2-inch-wide (1.3 cm) paintbrush

Hot glue gun and glue sticks

What You Do

1. Make sure you have enough canisters for each of the lights on the strand. If you need more, contact local photographers. They'll probably be happy to give their canisters to you.

2. Have a parent help you drill holes in the bottom of each of the canisters. Start with a drill bit that looks like it's just a little smaller than the light. Once the hole is drilled in the center of the canister's bottom, check to see if the light fits through the hole. If it doesn't, use a slightly larger drill bit to make the hole wider. Keep doing this until you can thread the light through the hole.

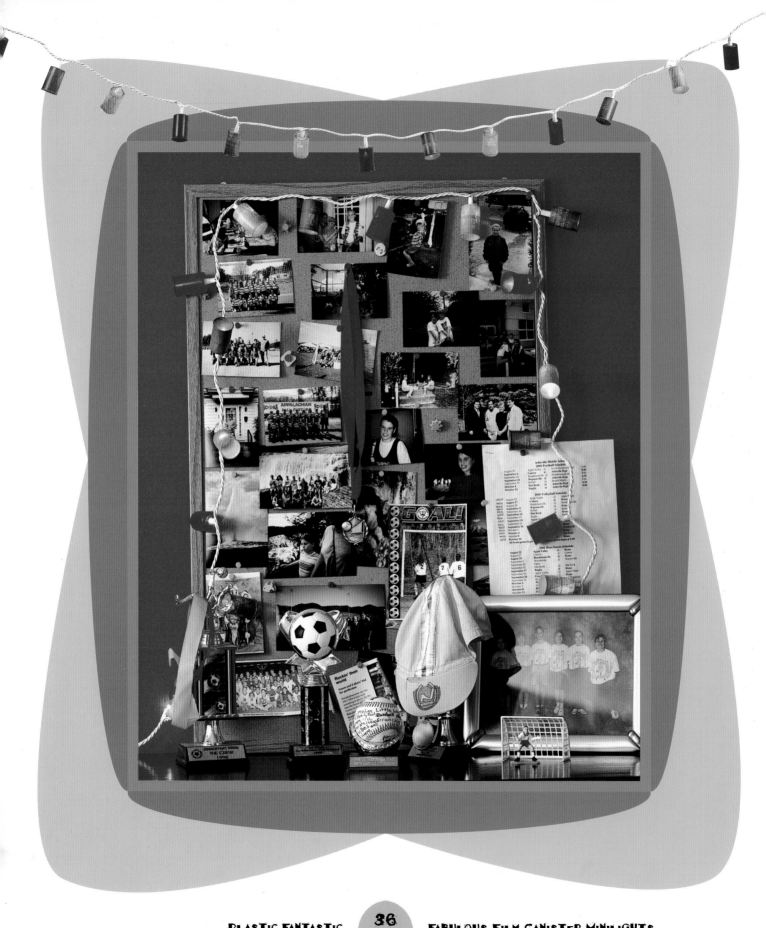

3. To decorate the canisters, trace the bottom of one canister (including the hole you made) on a piece of the colored tissue paper. Trace one circle for each of the canisters being used. Cut out all of the circles (and the hole in each one) with the scissors. Set the circles aside.

4. Take another sheet of the tissue paper and cut it into strips that are roughly 2 inches (5 cm) wide and 4½ inches (11.4 cm) long to wrap around the canisters. You'll need two strips for every canister.

5. Work on one film canister at a time. Use the paintbrush to spread a layer of the decoupage glue over the outside of the canister. Wrap a strip of the colored tissue paper around the canister, above the rim, and use your fingertips to smooth out any air bubbles or wrinkles between the paper and the canister. Wrap all of the canisters in this way. When you've covered all of the canisters and they feel dry, glue a second layer of paper around each one.

6. Cut ¼-inch-wide (6 mm) strips of tissue paper long enough to wrap around the rim of each canister. For each canister, spread glue around the rim, inside and out. Press the thin paper strip around the rim and fold the extra paper inside the rim. Smooth the paper in place with your fingertips.

7. Glue the paper circles to the outside bottoms of the canisters. Smooth out any air bubbles or wrinkles as you press each paper circle in place.

8. Brush a final coat of the decoupage glue over the outsides of the canisters and just inside the rims to seal the paper layers.

9. Push each canister over a mini-light so the base of the light fits in the canister hole. If the hole is a little too big, use a dab of hot glue in the hole to stick the canister to the lightbulb base.

Mini-light Tips

To hang your new mini-lights, drape the strand over well-spaced hooks or tacks. For safety, don't separate the individual wires or split them over the hooks.

Most sets of mini-lights come with a special red bulb, which an adult can help you install, to make them blink.

Don't be fooled by their tiny bulbs, mini-lights do get hot after they've been on for awhile. Be certain to unplug them after a couple of hours and anytime you leave your room.

RECYCLED BOOKMARKS

Floppy disks are known for getting corrupted, and many a kid has lost a homework assignment because of a bad disk. But, with a little creative destruction you can alter that bad disk to make a bookmark that's guaranteed to hold your place.

What You Need

Old 3½-inch (8.9 cm) computer diskettes

Butter knife

Heavy-duty scissors

Permanent marker

Acrylic paint or markers

Paintbrush

Fabric in solid colors and with patterns, faux fur, or felt*

Glue

* You can also glue photos, stickers, and fake gemstones, or use stamps and permanent ink to decorate your bookmarks.

What You Do

1. Place the diskette on a flat surface and use the buttter knife to pry off the metal clip that protects the diskette.

2. Pry apart the corners of the diskette by sliding the knife inside the opening where the metal clip was.

3. Remove the inside parts of the diskette and save them in your craft box for future projects. Leave the diskette square, or cut it in half with scissors to make narrower bookmarks for paperback books.

4. Draw a design on the diskette case with the permanent markers. Color in your design with the acrylic paint or markers.

5. If you want to cover your bookmark with fabric, set the diskette on the fabric you want to use as the background layer. Use a brightly colored marker to trace an outline of the diskette onto the fabric. Cut the fabric around the outline you drew, and check to see that the fabric fits the bookmark. Double the length of the fabric to cover both sides of the diskette.

6. Spread a thin layer of glue on the diskette and smooth the fabric onto the plastic. Be sure you don't cover the open end of the diskette. You can cut out designs in other pieces of fabric and glue them on top of the background layer to make a picture. Follow these same steps for gluing a photo to the diskette.

7. Slip the open end of your new bookmark onto the pages of your latest book, and let it keep your place until you have time to read again.

SECRET JOURNAL

CD cases make the perfect covers for secret journals that hide your private thoughts from snoops. And your writings and sketches will be safe inside the plastic case, even on those occasions when you tear your room apart in search of missing sneakers or lost library books. Use paints as we did here, or come up with your own design of mixed materials that inspires you to open the case and pen your thoughts inside.

What You Need

CD case

Scrap paper

Permanent marker

Acrylic paint

Paintbrush

Metallic paper

Compact disk (CD)

Pencil

Scissors

Glue

What You Do

1. Remove the cover art from the CD case. You'll need to carefully remove the inside plastic where the CD usually sits in order to take out the back art. Draw several designs on scrap paper until you find one that you really like. Draw your favorite design with the marker on all sides of the CD case.

2. Fill in the design with the paint and let the case dry. You may want to apply a second coat of paint after the first has dried com-

pletely. Instead of paint, you can use permanent markers, or you can glue a collage of pictures to the covers.

3. Make the booklet that will go inside the case the same way you'd make paper dolls or a string of snowflakes. Fold the metallic paper like an accordion so it's as wide as the CD (figure 1).

4. Trace the edge and inner circle of the CD onto the folded stack of paper so the edge of the CD lines up with each side of the paper (figure 2).

5. Hold the folded paper together with one hand and cut the CD shape from it with the other. Be sure to leave 1 inch (2.5 cm) of the paper uncut on the left and right sides of the stack so the folded paper stays connected (figure 3).

6. Set the booklet in the case and trim it to fit like a real CD. Glue the last

Fig. 1

Fig. 2

Fig. 3

page to the inside of the case (where the CD would go) so it doesn't fall out.

Flat Tire Picture Frames

Flats. They'll make you want to heave your perfectly good bike into the street for the garbage truck to run over. But flat tires don't have to be a downer. This project transforms them into new, mini-picture frames for all your cool photos.

What You Need

Old bike tire inner tubes

Scissors

Photographs

Cardboard

Glue or tape

Stamps, paints, embossing powder, and/or 3-D paints

What You Do

1. Locate the metal valve on the tire tube. Use the scissors to cut the tube on each side of the valve to create the rectangular frame. (The size is up to you.)

2. Center the tire rectangle over a favorite photograph, and trace the edges of the tire onto the part of the picture you want framed (figure 1). Cut out the rectangle from the rest of the photograph.

3. Place the tire frame over a piece of cardboard, and trace the edges of the tire frame onto the cardboard. Cut the cardboard a little bit smaller than the frame so it'll fit inside it.

4. Cut a rectangle out of the front of the tube to create a border that's a little smaller than the actual photo (figure 2).

5. Center the photo on the cardboard so it lines up the way you want it to in the frame. Use glue or tape to hold the photo to the cardboard in this position. Slide the cardboard and photo into the rubber frame (figure 3).

Fig. 1

6. You can leave the frame the way it is, or use stamps and paints, or glue small objects in place, to decorate it. To make a name tag for the frame, decorate a small piece of rubber with letter stamps and embossing powder or 3-D paint, and glue in place.

7. Don't think you have to throw away the rest of the tube. You can make a bunch of frames without the valve as a backing by simply gluing small magnets to the backs of the tube frames. Voila—perfect mini-frames for the fridge!

Fig. 2

Fig. 3

METAL
madness

Metal is wondrous stuff. It falls from space as meteorites, bubbles up from the Earth's iron core, and rests in the

rock beneath mountains. It's a natural part of our world, adding color to the landscape around us and to artists' canvasses—as ingredients in paint and crayon colors (hence the names cobalt blue and zinc white). We use it for money, wear it as jewelry, and rely on it to hold up our tallest buildings and carry us to Mars (called the Red Planet because its surface contains so much iron).

Metal also makes people do strange things. Need proof? How about the Yukon and Alaska Goldrush of the 1800s when millions of men and women risked their lives traveling thousands of miles by foot, horse, and boat for the chance that they

might find a shiny nugget of gold in a cold stream. And if someone told you they had a hunch that there was a load of silver buried in your backyard, you'd probably be out there with a shovel tomorrow, digging up every patch of grass to find it—your neighbor's dog would be so envious.

Unfortunately, our desire for metal has left huge scars on the Earth where mountains have been flattened, rivers altered, and enormous pits dug to get at

metal-rich rock. Processing metal ore into finished shiny sheets and slabs requires enormous amounts of energy, mostly from coal and oil, the burning of which adds to air pollution, acid rain, and global warming. It's a good thing metal is also easy to recycle; salvaged scrap metal is a regular ingredient in new steel and aluminum. And if you've ever helped with a bottle and can drive for a school or charity, you know that recycling metal is a moneymaker.

Crafty kids all over the world have figured out ways to turn discarded metal into new toys, decorations, and drums for themselves or to sell to admirers. Here's your chance, and you won't need a blowtorch or fancy equipment. Start small with scissors, glue, and the cans, foil, bottlecaps, wire, and scraps of metal that take up space in your trash to make cool things for yourself and others. We'll even show you how to make your own tin can xylophone with instructions from a musician who's an expert at coaxing music from all sorts of trash. Once you learn from these projects, we're sure you'll come up with a gazillion more uses for old metal.

THE ABSOLUTELY FABULOUS, ONE-OF-A-KIND, DINOSAUR GRIDDLE CLOCK

ADULT ASSISTANCE NECESSARY

This project proves that you can make a clock out of almost anything. Some clocks can be put together with glue, others may require a drill, but ultimately a cool, wacky clock only needs a little imagination.

What You Need

Old frying pan

Template on page 141

Use of a photocopy machine or scanner (see page 8)

Marker

Drill with a $^1\!/_4$-inch (6 mm) bit

Plastic dinosaurs or any old plastic toys

Hot glue gun and glue sticks

Clockworks and clock hands (available at craft stores)

Batteries (check clockworks instructions for what kind you need)

What You Do

1. Enlarge the template on page 141 to fit the bottom of the frying pan. Poke a hole in the center of the template and make a dot on the frying pan with the marker at this center point.

2. With help from an adult, drill a ¼-inch-diameter (6 mm) hole through the dot you just made in the center of the pan.

3. Turn the pan over, and line the hole in the template with the hole in the frying pan. Make a dot with the marker on the bottom of the pan at each of the hour points on the template.

4. Use hot glue to attach your plastic figures in place around the frying pan to mark the hours. You may want to put your largest object at 12 o'clock.

5. Follow the diagram on the package of clockworks to install them in your clock. This is the big moment when your frying pan will transform into a terrific timekeeper. Set the hands in place on the clock as shown on the package. Put the battery in the back of the case, and listen for the telltale tick-tock of a bonafide clock.

Cool Non-Metallic Variation

Make a glow-in-the-dark CD clock with some 3-D paints and another set of clock-works. After you paint the CD, use the template on page 141 to create your original time markers on the CD. When the paint on the CD is dry, assemble the clockworks. Squeeze some hot glue around the shaft on the battery case. Look for the triangular indent or hang tag on the back of the battery case and line up the top of the triangle with 12 o'clock on the CD. Press the battery case against the back of the CD, then set the clock aside until the glue has set.

WHAT ELSE CAN BECOME A CLOCK?

Old record albums

Vegetable steamers

A hat

A plate

An old sink stopper

Photographs glued to foam core

An old book

A piece of driftwood

A lunchbox

A game board (use the pieces of the game as the time markers)

A plastic cup

Anything you can drill a hole into!

Kokopelli Candleholders

Ancient drawings of Kokopelli, the flute playing figure, dance on cave walls in the American Southwest. Native Anasazi legends of the region describe Kokopelli as a musical spirit who traveled the land bringing good fortune, music, dance, and a little mischief to the people he met. Imagine lying on your floor after a tough day at school and watching the light from your own Kokopelli-inspired candleholders dance around your ceiling. Maybe some good fortune will come your way.

What You Need

3 empty, clean metal cans

Template on page 141

White paper and pencil

Tape

Marker (optional)

Towel

Hammer and nail

Spray paint (look for varieties made for metal)

3 small votive candles

What You Do

1. Fill the cans with water and put them in the freezer overnight. This will keep the cans from denting when you hammer the nail into them to make the design.

2. Make three copies of the template on page 141. Tape the templates to the cans, or draw the design on each can with a marker.

3. Place the first can on top of a towel that's been placed on your work table. Put the other two cans back in the freezer.

4. Hammer the nail into the dots on the template. If the ice in the can starts to melt, refreeze it.

5. When you've outlined your design with nail holes, place the can in the sink until

the ice melts. If the bottom of the can has bulged out from freezing, turn the can upside down on the floor and use the hammer to tap it flat again. Repeat this process with the other cans.

6. When the cans are dry, take them outdoors to paint them with the spray paint.

7. Place the candleholders on a solid surface well away from any walls, curtains, and other flammable materials. Use small candles, and never leave them burning when you're not in the room. Remember to keep lit candles out of the reach of pets and little kids.

Super Stylin' Desk Set

Back-to-school means new pens, pencils, computer disks, art supplies, and more, but where to keep it all? Instead of buying an ordinary desk organizer, make cool-looking containers like these with spray paint, yarn, and old cans. Best of all, you'll be able to make a desk organizer that's a perfect fit for your desk and your stuff.

What You Need

Assorted, clean, metal cans

Steel wool or sandpaper

Newspapers

Spray paint (look for varieties made for metal)

Washable glue

Yarn

Scissors

Damp rag

What You Do

1. Use steel wool on each can to rub off any rust, old label glue, and to scratch up the surface so the paint will stick better when you apply it.

2. Set the cans on newspapers outdoors, and coat the insides and outsides of the cans with the spray paint. Let them dry.

3. Spread a thin layer of glue all the way around the center of one of the cans, then wrap the yarn around it, over the glue. Repeat for the rest of the cans. Instead of yarn, you can glue paper or fabric to the cans, or paint them with 3-D paints for decoration.

4. When you've finished decorating the cans, use a damp rag to rub off any obvious glue smudges that you see.

SODA CAN BUG

Aluminum cans are so thin: an ordinary pair of scissors is all you need to cut them up and begin creating. So go ahead and make your own version of a soda can bug to hang around the house or surprise someone in your family.

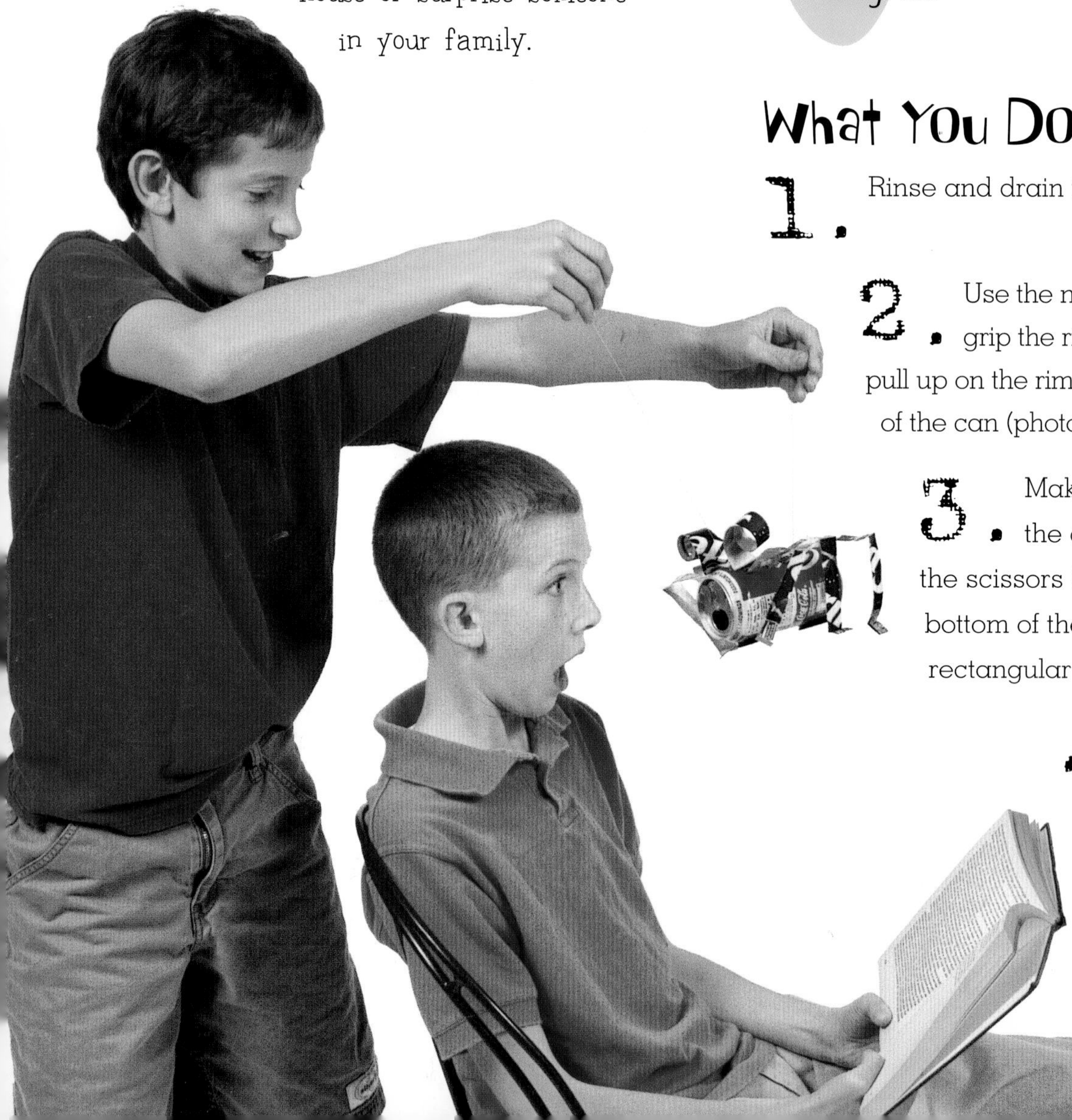

What You Need

2 aluminum cans

Needle-nose pliers

Scissors

Hot glue gun and glue sticks

Pencil

Sequins, buttons, or beads for eyes

Fishing line

What You Do

1. Rinse and drain the aluminum cans.

2. Use the needle-nose pliers to grip the rim of the first can, then pull up on the rim to tear it from the rest of the can (photo 1).

3. Make a slit from the top of the can to its bottom with the scissors (photo 2). Cut off the bottom of the can so you have a rectangular piece of aluminum.

4. Cut the aluminum rectangle into eight ½-inch-wide (1.3 cm) strips for the legs of your bug. Bend each metal strip at its center and also near one end to make the leg joints.

5. Squeeze a dab of hot glue on the straight end of the leg (not the foot end) and press the leg against the second soda can (photo 3). Repeat for each of the legs.

6. Cut two small triangles from a leftover piece of aluminum to make fangs or antennae. Wrap each triangle around the pencil to give it a curl, then attach them to your bug with hot glue. Glue beads, buttons, or sequins in place as eyes and elsewhere on the body for extra features.

7. Hang your bug by attaching a piece of fishing line to the top of the body with hot glue. You can also glue a piece of magnet to the bottom of the body to hold your creature to any metal surface or use hook and loop tape to stick it to furniture.

1

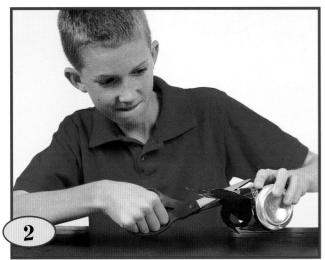

2

3

HANDY-DANDY DENIM WALLET

Pull that old pair of jeans out of the bottom of your dresser drawer and turn it into a wallet you can use to store the money you'll need for a new pair of jeans.

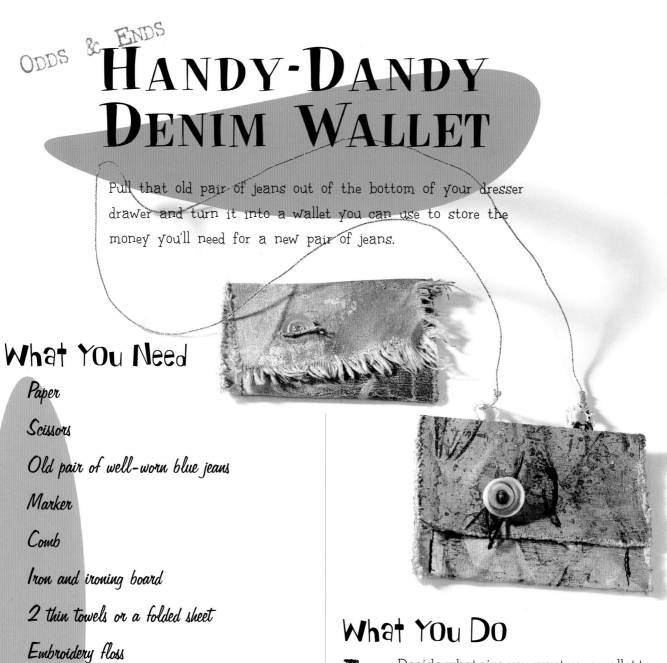

What You Need

Paper

Scissors

Old pair of well-worn blue jeans

Marker

Comb

Iron and ironing board

2 thin towels or a folded sheet

Embroidery floss

Large sewing needle

Button

Acrylic or latex paints and paintbrush (optional)

Strap (optional)

What You Do

1. Decide what size you want your wallet to be. Consider the sorts of things you want to keep in your wallet and how you want to carry it. Do you want it to fit in a pocket, or do you want to put a strap on it and wear it as a bag?

2. Create a pattern by cutting a piece of paper and folding it into an envelope the same size you want for your wallet (figure 1).

3. Lay your jeans out flat on a table or the floor. Open the paper pattern and trace around it with the marker onto one of the pant legs. Follow the outline and cut the fabric from the jeans.

4. Fray the edges of the fabric either by washing and drying it or by setting the fabric on a table and dragging a comb along the edges. Trim any extra-long strings.

5. Lay the fabric on the ironing board between the two thin towels or folded sheet. Press the fabric flat with the hot iron. Fold the fabric into the shape of the envelope pattern so the top of the fabric folds over the bottom of the fabric to close the wallet.

6. Use the embroidery floss and large needle to sew the sides of the wallet together (figures 2, 3). Trim off any extra thread when you've finished sewing the seams.

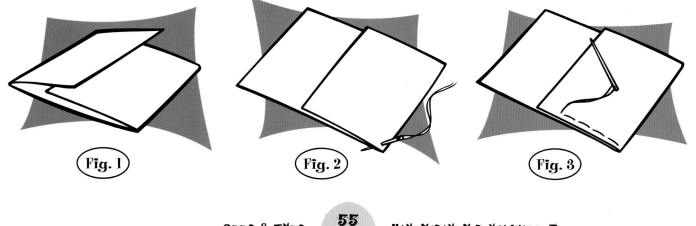

Fig. 1   Fig. 2   Fig. 3

7. Hold the wallet so you're looking at the side with the flap. Use the scissors to cut a slit (wide enough to fit the button through), centered, and at least a ½ inch (1.3 cm) from the bottom edge of the flap (figure 4). Close the flap against the bottom of the wallet and make a dot with the marker through the slit on the fabric below. Sew (or have an adult help you sew) the button over the mark you just made (figures 5, 6, 7).

8. A seashell, bead, or any small object you can fit a piece of thread through can become an instant button. Make a slit in the flap just as you did for a regular button, but use the object you've chosen as a guide for the size. Make two holes in the bottom half of the wallet, under the slit in the flap, as far apart as the length of the object. Pass the thread through one of the holes, then through your object, and back into the second hole. Pull the thread tightly and tie the ends together in a knot, close to the fabric, on the inside of the wallet.

9. Paint over your wallet with acrylic or latex paint if you want. When the paint has dried completely, machine wash and dry your wallet with a load of old towels or sheets. The paint will make the jeans even more durable, and it looks pretty cool too.

10. Turn the wallet into a bag by adding a strap. To do so, punch a hole through the fabric in each of the top corners on the back of the purse. Poke each end of the strap into the holes and tie knots in each end to keep the strap from slipping out of the holes. For a fancier strap, slide beads, shells, or other decorations onto the strap before attaching it to the wallet.

Fig. 4

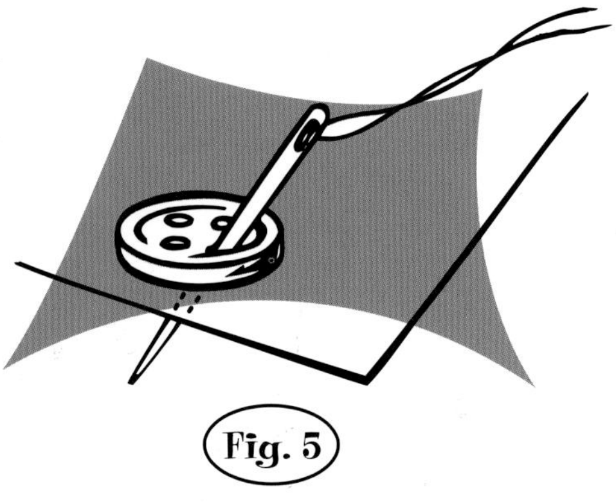

Fig. 5

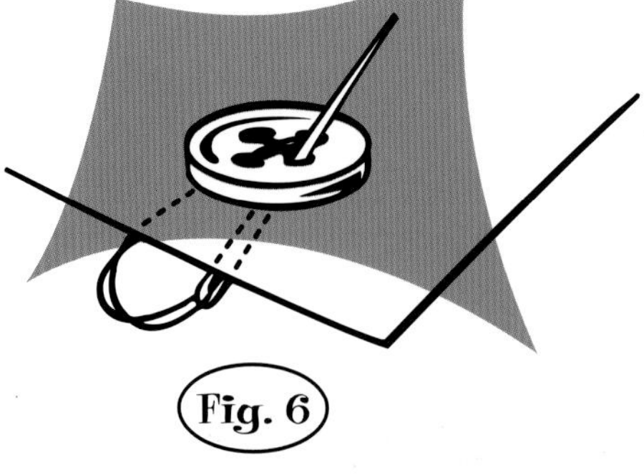

Fig. 6

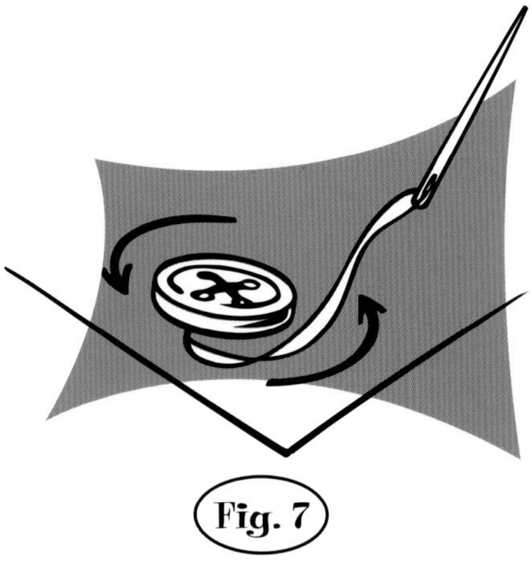

Fig. 7

PRESENTING... THE WORLD'S FAVORITE METAL... ALUMINUM

Aluminum is the most common metal on the planet, and we use it everywhere—in our houses, for our cars, and even in our armpits. (It's an ingredient in deodorant.) Our favorite metal requires 4 tons (3.6 t) of raw bauxite, mined as a mineral from the Earth's crust, and thousands of kilowatts of electricity to produce each ton of new aluminum. The bulk of the nearly 135 million tons (122 million t) of bauxite ore produced each year comes from mines in Australia, Jamaica, Brazil, and Guinea.

Aluminum is 100 percent recyclable, and remelting it saves 95 percent of the resources used to make new metal. Aluminum cans are easy to recycle, and some stores even pay you for your empties. But what to do with aluminum foil? Call the recycling center closest to your town and find out what they accept and how much they pay for it. Most also accept pie plates, oven liners, and other versions of foil. The following are a few unusual ways you can reuse and recycle aluminum foil. Just remember to clean any food bits off of it before you use it.

1. With your principal's permission, challenge your school to make a giant aluminum foil ball, then roll it over to a recycler. Use the money the ball earns to make a donation to an Earth-friendly organization.

2. Origami isn't just for paper; try making a mobile with foil cranes.

3. Turn your bedroom into a planetarium by covering a window with several sheets of aluminum foil taped together. Poke holes in the aluminum foil in the shape of constellations and other galactic features. Sunlight will shine through the holes to illuminate the pinhole stars.

4. Amaze your friends with your skill as an aluminum foil sculptor.

5. Make a mini-thermos out of an ordinary bottle or can by wrapping aluminum around it to keep your drink cold longer.

6. Make foil beads. See page 77 for bead-making instructions.

7. Don't bother buying metallic papers; use aluminum foil for art projects, such as making cards or covering cardboard picture frames.

8. Scrunch aluminum foil into a ball to use as a hackey-sack, baseball, or basketball.

9. Design ornaments to hang in your window and reflect light around your room.

10. Make an aluminum foil beanie, a form-fitting cap some people believe helps to deflect mind-controlling waves. Wear one to see if it blocks your sister's evil eye.

CANDY TIN TRAVEL GAMES

Metal candy tins are perfect containers for holding your own version of magnetic poetry or a favorite travel game. Or, fill your tin with foreign words and phrases for a fun way to study for your next vocabulary quiz.

What You Need

Old magazines or books

Use of a photocopy machine (optional)

Scissors

Metal candy tin

100-grit sandpaper

3-D paint

Acrylic paints and paintbrush

Newspapers

Clear acrylic spray enamel

Self-adhesive magnetic sheets (available at craft stores)

Tweezers

What You Do

1. First, you need to collect words. Photocopy text from books (we used a Spanish language book) or cut words from the pages of old magazines. You could even type a list of your favorite words, print them, and cut them up.

2. Use the 100-grit sandpaper to scrub the old paint off of the candy tin. Draw a border around the lid with the 3-D paint, and decorate the tin with acrylic paint.

3. Set the tin on newspapers outdoors, and spray it with the clear acrylic enamel. This prevents the new paint from chipping.

4. Peel the paper backing off of the magnetic sheet and set the sheet down so the sticky side faces up. Use the tweezers to lift the words you've cut out and stick them to the magnetic sheet.

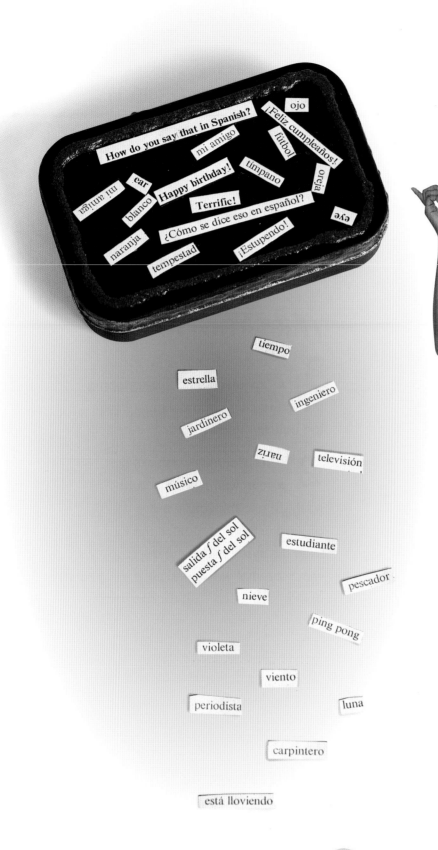

5. Cut the words from the magnetic sheet and store them in the tin.

Not into poetry or studying for your next Spanish test? Make miniature versions of chess, checkers, or a favorite board game to keep in your tin. Design the game board with tiny strips of black tape on top of the tin to host your competitions.

MAKE YOUR OWN LAMP

You can easily make your own lamp with a kit from a craft or home supply store and an olive oil can for the base. Once you get the hang of it, you may want to experiment with old toys or shoes as lamp bases too. Your family will be amazed by your Edison-like bright ideas. Give your funky lamps to friends and family members as gifts, and remember to include an energy-saving, lightbulb with your package.

What You Need

Tin olive oil can

Pliers

Clip-on lampshade

Acrylic paint and paintbrush

Hammer and large nail

Lamp kit

Energy-saving lightbulb (choose a style to match the clip on your lampshade)

What You Do

1. If the can has a plastic spout, remove it by gripping it with the pliers and pulling it from the hole in the can.

2. Thoroughly wash out the can with hot water and soap. Shake the soapy water around in the can to rinse the oil from the sides. Rinse out the can with more hot water and set it upside down in a dish rack to dry.

3. Meanwhile, paint the outside of the lampshade in a color to match the olive oil can, and set it aside to dry.

4. When the can is clean and dry, make a hole in it for the electrical cord near the

bottom of the side that won't be visible. Set the can so the side you want the hole in is facing up, then punch the nail through the side of the can with the hammer.

5. Read the instructions on the lamp kit package, and assemble the lamp. Ask an adult to check the assembly.

6. Screw the lightbulb into the lamp socket and plug in the cord to make sure your lamp works. If it doesn't light up, unplug the cord and check all of the lamp's connections.

7. Clip the painted lampshade onto the lightbulb and set up your lamp wherever you can use a little more light.

20 Simple Things You Can Do to Be Earth Friendly

1. Reduce the amount of stuff you buy, and look for things that are sold in recyclable packaging. Think about how many uses you'll get out of that new item and whether you can make it yourself before you buy it.

2. Recycle everything you can, and reuse the things you can't.

3. Replace the lightbulbs in your house with energy-efficient bulbs. Turn off all lights and appliances when you're not using them.

4. Compost your food waste (see page 102).

5. Host a yard sale to get rid of the things you don't want but someone else might. Have a school yard sale to raise money for programs and activities.

6. Don't ask your parents for a ride to soccer practice. Walk, ride, or roll powered by your own two feet.

7. Grow some of your family's favorite vegetables in large pots, or plant a garden.

8. Organize a stream clean-up in your area.

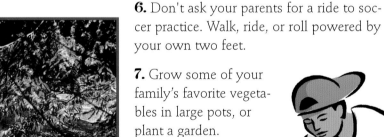

9. Help an elderly neighbor prepare her trash for recycling.

10. Bring your own bags to the grocery store so you don't have to use new plastic or paper bags.

11. Save trees by using rags instead of paper towels for all your chores.

12. Be an activist. Write letters about environmental issues to the editor of your local newspaper as well as government officials.

13. Plant a tree; trees are the lungs of the planet.

14. Adopt an acre of rainforest or sponsor a wild animal through an organization such as The Nature Conservancy, Friends of the Earth, World Wildlife Fund, or Save-the-Whales.

15. Your great-grandpa was right, use handkerchiefs. A soft handkerchief saves your nose when you have a bad cold, and it doubles as a rag when you have a spill. It lets you have an instant game of capture the flag, and saves countless numbers of trees from being cut down to make tissues.

16. Host a book swap at your yard sale, or donate old books to a library, nursing home, school, or resource center.

17. Take a field trip to the grocery store or a local farmer's market and look for organic foods (which are grown without chemical pesticides and fertilizers) to sample and buy.

18. Be an eco-detective. Search the Internet and newspapers for news about environmental issues.

19. Buy and use rechargeable batteries. They last many times longer and pollute less than disposable batteries.

20. Save water. Challenge your family to see who can take the shortest shower. Keep the water off while brushing your teeth or washing dishes, and help your parents fix any leaky faucets in your house. Some cities give out free kits loaded with water-saving devices. See if the water authority in your community will give you one to install in your home.

TRASH TUNES

International recording artist Billy Jonas is no ordinary musician; he has a special talent for making music from trash! His traveling, one-man band includes giant plastic barrels, milk jugs, tin cans, bottlecaps, home-made mallets, and unusual creations including the "boingo-bongo xylophone" made with plastic containers and bed-springs.

Billy's fascination with making instruments out of everyday stuff started when he was just a kid banging pots, pans, and metal cans. Seeing a chance to encourage his talent (and save their cookware), his parents signed

him up for piano lessons. By eight years old he was playing guitar, and by 10, he had moved on to trombone. But by high school, he was back to banging pots and pans and creating instruments from found objects.

Through his CDs, videos, campfire sing-a-longs, school work-shops, and music hall performances, Billy Jonas teaches others that "music can happen anywhere, any-time, with anyone, and anything." So gather your metal cans, milk jugs, and odds and ends to assemble your own Billy Jonas-style band. We'll even give you a few tips for getting started and ideas for playing with friends.

TIN CAN XYLOPHONE

The first human attempt to make music may have been as simple as a rhythmic jam of smacking lips, clapping hands, and tapping feet. Throw in a couple of sticks as mallets and a mastodon skull for a base, and you've got yourself the makings of a prehistoric drumming circle. Today, all you need to start drumming is a group of tin cans and some rubber bands. But don't stop there! Once you make some mallets, take them on a tour of your house to uncover other suitable drum bases.

What You Need

Clean tin cans with the tops removed, in assorted sizes

Coffee can or similar large can

Pliers

2 pencils with erasers

Extra large rubber bands (different colors if possible)

Duct tape

What You Do

1. Examine the can rims for sharp pieces or "burrs" left over from the lids. Use the pliers to flatten the sharp pieces against the can so that they'll be safe to handle.

2. Test the cans to find those that make the best sounds. Set the cans on the floor with their bottoms up. Loosely hold one pencil in your hand like a drumstick, and tap each can with the eraser end of the pencil. If you don't like the sound of a can, put it back in the recycling bin. If you do like the sound, set it to the side to use for the xylophone. Organize the good cans in a line from highest to lowest pitch, or leave them unorganized for a random musical mix.

3. Turn all of the cans right-side up (so the bottoms are on the floor) and place them in a circle around the larger coffee can. Keep the cans in the same order you decided on in step 2.

4. Count the cans to figure out how many rubber bands you'll need. Use one rubber band for every three cans. We used 12 cans for this xylophone and four rubber bands to hold it all together. Stretch the rubber bands before assembling the xylophone.

5. Slide all of the rubber bands around the coffee can, and roll them almost to the can's bottom. Leave a space about as wide as your pinky, between each of the rubber bands.

6. Pull the lowest rubber band out and away from the coffee can and slide it over one of the smaller cans. Let the rubber band snap back, so it holds the smaller can tightly against the big can. Repeat with the next can and the next higher rubber band (figure 1). Once you've stretched each of the rubber bands around a can, start over with the first rubber band to attach the rest of the cans. If you have a really big rubber band, you can stretch it around all of the cans like a belt to hold them together.

7. Carefully turn the whole arrangement upside down, so that the can bottoms face up and the open ends are on the floor. (It should look like a mushroom.) Adjust all of the cans so the bottoms are even with the bottom of the central can. If any of the cans slip, add more rubber bands or wrap duct tape around the whole thing.

8. Pick up your mallets and…drum roll, please…bang out your own tin can beat.

Fig. 1

9. To get an even better sound out of your xylophone, twist a rubber band around the eraser end of each pencil for maximum mallet potential (figure 2). When playing, hold your mallets as loosely as possible to produce the clearest sound.

Fig. 2

Did Ya Know…

Tin cans are mostly made of steel and only coated with tin. Test whether a food can is made of steel or aluminum by holding a magnet to it. The magnet will stick to the steel can.

THE BILLY JONAS JUGUITAR

If you sing in the shower or tap pencils on the desk while doing your homework, you just may have the makings of a rock star. Get started on the road to musical stardom by combining a bow with a plastic jug base for an easy-to-play juguitar. And, um,...will you send us a postcard when you hit the big time?

What You Need

Wooden measuring stick
(yardstick or meter stick)

Saw, file, or pocketknife

5 feet (1.5 m) nylon cord
(available at hardware stores)

Chair

Plastic milk jug

Scissors

Colored tape, markers, and paints to
decorate with (optional)

What You Do

1. Gently bend the measuring stick back and forth to make it more flexible.

2. Get an adult to help use the saw, file, or pocketknife to cut a small, V-shape notch in the center of both ends of the measuring stick. Then cut notches on both sides of the measuring stick, 2 to 3 inches (5 to 7.6 cm) from each end (figure 1).

3. Tightly wrap the cord around one end of the measuring stick, so it catches in both of the side notches. Tie the cord together with a knot, and pull the long end of the cord up and over the top edge of the measuring stick (figure 2).

4. Hold the long end of the cord in one hand and the stick in the other. Flip the measuring stick upside down, so the end with the knot is near the floor. Sit down in the chair and hook your foot under the bottom end of the measuring stick so that it can't slide around. Gently curve the measuring stick to form a bow (figure 3).

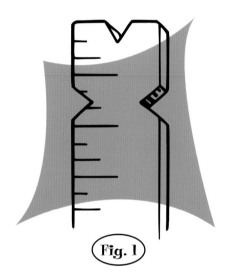
Fig. 1

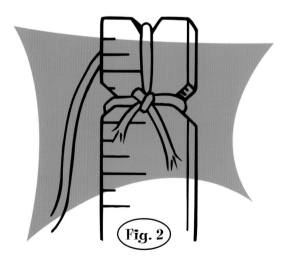
Fig. 2

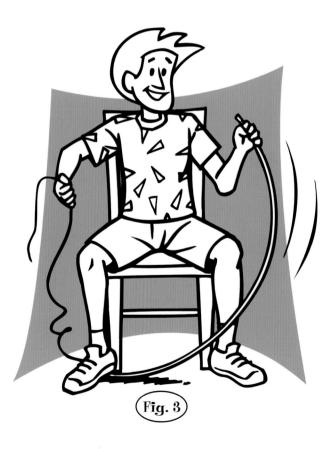
Fig. 3

Bend the bow back and forth with one hand to tighten and slacken the string while plucking the string with your other hand.

5. Pull the cord tightly over the top of the measuring stick and through the notch. Wrap the string around the measuring stick so it catches in the side notches, and tie a knot to hold it in place. Wrap the rest of the string around the end of the measuring stick a few more times, then tie it again. If the string stretches and the bow straightens, bend the measuring stick again and retie the cord.

6. Once you've made a good bow that will hold its shape, push the end (without the excess hanging string) down into the bottom of the milk jug.

7. Start jammin'. You'll have to experiment to find your favorite way to play the juguitar, but here are a few techniques that we found work well.

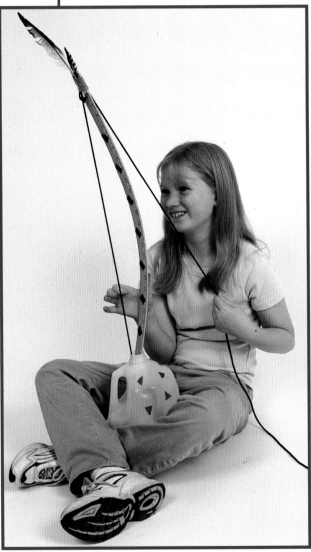

Hold the juguitar upright and pull the loose string to bend the bow back and forth. Pluck the bow string like you're playing a harp.

WHERE YOUR TRASH ENDS UP

You throw things away everyday, but do you know where "away" is? Follow this diagram to see where your garbage really goes when you throw it away.

Gases and smoke particles from incinerators are linked to poor air quality, smog, and global warming.

Air pollution mixes with water vapor in clouds and falls to Earth in rain and snow. Acid rain damages forests, lakes, crops, and soil.

Garbage is sent to incinerators where it is burned. The leftover toxic ash must be carefully disposed of.

Rotting trash produces methane gas, which is a greenhouse gas and air pollutant.

Garbage is dumped in landfills where it slowly decomposes.

Recycling, reusing, and composting reduce garbage.

Runoff from landfills can pollute groundwater.

PAPER
works

Walk around your house and note how many things are made from paper: this book, and the ones on your bookshelf, birthday cards, telephone books, paper towels, photographs, tea bags, tissues, bumper stickers, playing cards, board games, toilet paper, and on and on. The demand for paper is enormous! The United States alone produces 187 billion pounds (84 billion kg) of paper each year—that's 749 pounds (337 kg) of paper per person! Nowadays, we toss perfectly good, reusable sheets of paper in the trash without a

thought, but paper wasn't always so cheap and abundant.

For almost 2,000 years, paper was mostly made from old clothes, rags, and whatever plant materials were available, such as bark, hemp, and straw. But as more people learned to read and paper mills were built, papermakers struggled to find enough material to keep up with the demand. It wasn't until the French physicist and naturalist Rene Antoine Ferchault de Reaumura watched wasps spreading woody pulp on their papery hive that the idea for using plentiful trees to make paper seemed possible. Just a century ago, after a lot of messy experiments, papermakers finally figured out how to mix wood with water, chemicals, and heat to make paper.

Today, 10,000 paper mills around the world mash wood into paper and cardboard to make all of the products that surround you. But it's a resource-gobbling business: one ton (.9 t) of new paper requires 17 to 20 trees, plus water and energy, and the world uses 300 million tons (270 million t) of paper and cardboard each year. To supply a steady amount of wood to paper mills, forests are managed like rows of corn, chopped and replanted, fertilized, and treated with chemicals to fight wood-munching insects. As the demand for paper, cardboard, and lumber continues to rise, more and more forests are turning into tree farms. In fact, only 16 percent of the world's original forests have been left alone. That's bad news for the plants, animals, and people who depend on rich, natural forests for survival. And too much paper is simpy thrown away, ending up in landfills and incinerators.

Save forests, reduce air pollution, and help clean up the Earth by reusing and recycling paper and wood products. Choose recycled and tree-free papers for school assignments to reduce the demand for new wood. Plant a tree in your neighborhood, encourage paper recycling at school, and flip through the pages of this chapter to find alternative ways to reuse paper and cardboard. We'll show you how to turn a newspaper into a sturdy shelf for your room, make your own recycled paper from junk mail, and roll magazine pages into beads. And just wait till you see what you can do with an old pizza box.

HANDMADE PAPER & RECYCLED ENVELOPES

Imagine if you multiplied the amount of paper you use each day by the number of days in one school year, then by the number of kids in your school, and finally by the number of schools in your city. The number is so big your calculator can't even display it! Instead of buying new paper products, set up a papermaking factory right in your own kitchen to make your own line of letters, cards, and colorful, homemade envelopes.

What You Need

Used paper and scraps of all sorts, including colored construction paper, office paper, and wrapping paper

Blender

Dishpan or washtub

Window screen and matching picture frame to fit inside the dishpan*

Sponge (optional)

Thick wool blanket or felt

Old sheet

*You can also buy a papermaker's mold and deckle set (like the one used in this project) at most craft stores. The mold is the screen half of the set, and the deckle is the frame.

What You Do

1. Rip the paper into small pieces, no larger than your fingers. The smaller the pieces, the easier it will be for your blender to process the pulp. Place all of the pieces into the blender until it's three-quarters full. Fill the blender with water almost to the top.

2. Hold the lid on the blender while you press the pulse button off and on (photo 1). The water and paper will mix into a thick pulp. The pulp is ready to become paper when it looks like thick stew.

3. Fill the dish pan halfway to the top with water, then pour blender loads of pulp into the dish pan until it's three-quarters full (photo 2). You may need to make more pulp.

4. Hold the frame on top of the screen and dip them together into the pulp. Shake the screen gently back and forth to spread the pulp evenly over the surface of the screen (photo 3). Keep the screen and the frame level so the paper will have an even thickness.

5. Use your hand or a sponge to press some of the extra water out of the pulp on the mold. When the water has dripped out of the pulp, remove the frame and set it aside.

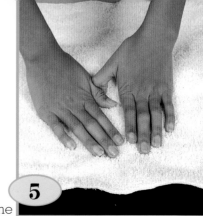

6. Quickly and steadily flip over the screen onto the blanket or piece of felt. Press against the back of the screen with your fingers or a sponge to release the paper to the fabric (photo 4).

7. Place the sheet over the fresh paper and press to get more of the water out of the pulp (photo 5). Flip over the fabric, paper, and sheet sandwich so the sheet is on the bottom, and carefully peel the fabric from the paper. Place the sheet with the fresh paper on it in a safe place to dry.

RECYCLED ENVELOPES

What You Need

Favorite pages from an old calendar or magazine

Scissors

Card or folded piece of stationery

Tape

Scrap white or other light-colored paper

Pen

Postage stamp

page (you want to put the best-looking side of the calendar page face down).

3. Fold the sides of the page over the edges of the card and crease the folds with your fingers. Fold the bottom of the page over the card.

4. Tape the sides of the folded page together to make a pocket, then fold down the top half of the paper to close the envelope. Use tape to seal the envelope.

5. Since your envelope is so colorful, cut a strip of the white paper to use as an address label so the mail carrier will be able to find the address easily. After writing the address on the paper, tape the paper, centered, on the front of the envelope.

What You Do

1. Trim one of the calendar pages so that the sides are even.

2. Center your card or folded piece of stationery on the back of the calendar

PAPER BEAD-IT

Reuse your family's old magazines and catalogs to make cool, colorful paper beads for all sorts of projects, including these one-of-a-kind necklaces.

What You Need

Magazines

Scissors

Pencil

Glue

String, elastic, or leather cord

Wooden, plastic, metal, or glass beads (optional)

What You Do

1. Tear colorful photos and advertisements from the pages of old magazines and catalogs.

2. Cut the pages into long triangles. Each bead will be as long as the base of the triangle, so for small beads, cut out narrow triangles, and for large beads, cut out wider triangles. Each triangle needs to be long enough to wrap around the pencil, plus 1 additional inch (2.5 cm) for gluing it in place.

3. To make a bead, center the pencil along the base of one of the triangles. Roll the paper around the pencil toward the triangle's tip. Stop rolling when you're about 1 inch (2.5 cm) from the tip. To make fatter beads, roll the paper triangles around markers, smooth sticks, paper towel tubes, or even a soda can.

4. Squeeze a thin layer of glue on the last inch of the paper triangle, and finish rolling the paper to its end. The glue will hold the bead together. Wipe any glue that seeps out from between the rolls of paper over the rest of the bead to seal and protect it.

5. When the glue has dried, slide the bead off the pencil. Follow steps 3 through 5 to make more beads.

6. Measure the elastic cord, string, or leather cord around your neck and cut it to the length you want it.

7. Slide the paper beads along the cord or string and alternate with wooden, plastic, metal, or glass beads for a more fancy necklace. You could also make bracelets or anklets by cutting some string or cord to fit around your wrist or ankle. After stringing all of the beads, tie the ends of the string or cord in a knot, and your necklace, anklet, or bracelet is ready to wear.

Did Ya Know?

Rainforests, the most diverse ecosystems on Earth, once covered 20 percent of the planet, but human activity and natural disasters have reduced them to just 6 percent and thousands of acres continue to be destroyed every day.

THE GREAT PAPER-BEAD RESOURCE PAGE

You can help reduce the demand for magazines and catalogs by canceling subscriptions for those your family never actually reads, and instead, look for articles and catalogs online or at the library. You can also swap issues with friends and neighbors. Donate old magazines to doctors' offices, libraries, nursing homes, or your classroom art closet. Recycle them to save landfill space and provide material for new paper. Or, cut them up and make more beads to use for crafting one of these cool projects:

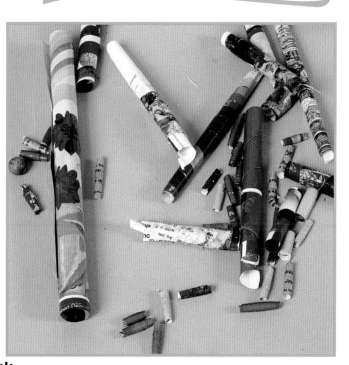

✳ **Shoelace decoration:** Slip a bead onto each end of your shoelace, and tie a knot in the shoelace to hold the bead in place.

✳ **Pencil and pen tops:** Tightly wrap beads on the pencil or pen, but don't slide them off afterwards.

✳ **Decoration for hair clips and hair ties:** Glue beads onto hair clips or make your own hair ties with elastic cord.

✳ **Picture frame design:** Glue beads around a plain frame.

✳ **Belt:** Make large beads and string them on rope to wrap around your wrist.

✳ **Doorway curtain:** Tie several beads onto colorful string, hold them in place with knots in the string, and hang the strings from a curtain rod.

✳ **Earrings:** Glue beads onto earring backs.

✳ **Bookmarks:** Slide beads onto a piece of leather cord that's longer than the book you're reading, and make a knot at each end of the cord.

✳ **Light pull:** Slip a large bead onto the end of a light chain and tie a knot at the base of the chain to hold the bead in place.

✳ **Zipper pull:** Wrap a bead around a zipper tag and use glue to help secure it in place.

✳ **Magnets:** Glue beads onto strips of magnets.

Did Ya Know?

According to the nonprofit organization, Conservatree, nearly 3 billion magazine issues a year are never even read. That's enough magazines to circle the Earth 20 times!

FLUTTER-BY BUTTERFLY FILTERS

Migrating butterflies and songbirds are disappearing as deforestation, modern farming practices, and the growth of cities reduce their food sources and habitats. Your family can support butterfly and bird habitats by selecting organic coffees, fruits, and vegetables at the grocery store. Then reuse your parents' coffee filters to make butterflies like these to decorate your windows or hang as a mobile to honor these amazing and endangered winged wildlife.

 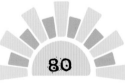

What You Need

Used coffee filters

Towel

Newspapers

Jars or cups

Water

Food coloring

2 to 4 eyedroppers

Colored pipe cleaners

Plastic colored beads

Fishing line or tape

What You Do

1. For several days, collect your parents' used coffee filters. Throw out or compost the old coffee grounds, and rinse the filters under cool water. Set the filters on the towel to dry.

2. Cover your work space with the newspapers so the food coloring won't stain the surface. Lay out the filters on top of the newspapers.

3. Fill each jar with about ¼ cup (60 mL) of water and add several drops of food coloring. You want the colors to be bright, especially the blue coloring, so they'll show up against the coffee stains on the filters.

4. Decorate the filters by squeezing drops of color from the eyedroppers to make patterns. Use separate eyedroppers for each color so the colors won't mix and turn brown. The drops of food coloring will expand through the filter, and wherever two or more colors meet, they'll mix to create a new shade. If you don't want the colors to mix as much, let each color dry before you add another.

5. When dry, fold each filter accordion style. Bend one of the pipe cleaners in half and wrap it around the center of one of the filters. Twist the pipe cleaner together to hold it in place.

6. Slip two of the beads down the twisted pipe cleaner to make the body of the butterfly.

7. Spread the filter apart to make the butterfly wings. Then spread the ends of the pipe cleaners apart (above the beads) to make the antennea.

8. Tie a piece of the fishing line below the beads on the pipe cleaners to hang each butterfly, or use tape to stick them to a surface.

PICK-UP STICKS

Picture life before TV, computer games, organized after-school sports, band practice, and movies. What did kids do? A game of pick-up sticks may seem a little dull compared to the high-tech games you have at your fingertips, but with a good group of friends, it can prove to be a fun way to pass the time. Reuse perfectly good wood skewers and an old cardboard tube to make your own version of this ancient game.

What You Need

- 30 used bamboo skewers (leftover from grilling shish kebabs)

- Soap and water

- Scissors

- Waxed paper

- Silver, green, purple, red, and yellow acrylic paints

- Paintbrush

- Clear acrylic spray enamel

- 1½-inch-diameter (3.8 cm) mailing tube, long enough to hold the skewers, with cap

- Pen or pencil

- Craft knife

- Piece of fabric as wide as the tube and long enough to wrap around it

- Craft glue

What You Do

1. Wash and dry the skewers with warm water and soap. If you want, use the scissors to snip off the very tip of the pointed end of the skewers so they won't be so sharp.

2. Spread the waxed paper on your work surface. Divide the skewers into piles and paint them as follows: 11 purple, 6 red, 6 yellow, 6 green, and 1 silver. Place the wet skewers on the waxed paper to dry.

3. When dry, carry the sticks outside on the piece of waxed paper, and spray them with the clear acrylic enamel.

4. Compare the length of the skewers with the length of the mailing tube and mark the top of the skewers on the tube with the pencil. Carefully cut the tube with the craft knife so it's long enough to hold the skewers when the cap is on it.

5. Cut the fabric to the length of the tube and wide enough so it wraps around the tube.

6. Spread glue on the outside of the tube with the paintbrush, and wrap the fabric around the tube. Brush extra glue onto the fabric where it overlaps itself, and press the two layers together. Also, spread extra glue around the ends of the tube so the fabric won't unravel over time.

How to Play Pick-Up Sticks

Native Americans are said to be the original inventors of pick-up sticks, at least in North America. European settlers learned the game from watching Native Americans play it with straws of wheat and have continued to pass it down through generations. There are many ways to play pick-up sticks, and we hope you'll invent your own rules. Here's one version to get you started.

1. Get two or three friends to play with you. Grab all of the sticks in one hand, and stand the handful on end on a flat surface. Open your hand, and let the sticks fall into a random pile on the floor or table.

2. One by one, each player tries to remove a stick from the pile without moving any of the other sticks. If a player moves any other stick, she must give up the rest of her turn and the next player goes. Any player who retrieves the silver stick can use it one time to separate two other sticks that are close together in the pile. This will make it easier for the player to pick up one of the sticks.

3. The game is over when all of the sticks have been picked up. Each player counts the number of sticks per color in their hand. You can assign any value you want to the stick colors, or follow this chart:

purple	**10** points
yellow	**15** points
red	**20** points
green	**25** points
silver	**50** points

There are many ways you can change the game to keep it interesting, such as changing the point system, the rules for using the silver stick, and even the number of sticks you play with. Make a list of the new rules you invent, and keep it in the tube for future games.

PLANT A TREE

Trees are the lungs of the planet; they help balance the gases in the atmosphere as they absorb carbon dioxide and release oxygen. One acre of trees absorbs 10,000 to 12,000 pounds (4,540 to 5,450 kg) of carbon dioxide and returns 8,000 pounds (3,630 kg) of fresh oxygen to the air. Their deep and vast root networks hold soil in place. They also drink up lots of water, purifying it and releasing it back into the environment slowly, over time. Trees breathe, they move, they eat and drink, and when a bunch of them get together as a forest, their actions control entire weather patterns. Trees lend us their twisted, leaf-covered branches for shade, and provide us with nuts, fruits, and medicines. Old-growth forests and rain forests provide homes to rare plants and animals. In fact,

70 percent of the creatures that live on land make their homes in forests. Unfortunately, we've managed to clear half of the world's forests, and continue to lose the rest at an alarming rate. So show some thanks to the trees and do the whole world a favor: plant a tree. Visit a local plant nursery for advice and supplies, and keep these tips in mind:

1. Choose a tree that naturally grows in your area. Consider a fruit or nut tree for tasty handpicked snacks.

2. Select a location for your tree where it will be allowed to safely grow for many years. Imagine it fully grown, and find a spot that will give it all the room it needs, above and below the ground.

3. Like pets, young trees need food and water to grow strong, and it even helps to talk to them regularly.

MEMORY MATCHBOXES

Turn an empty matchbox into a memory box for some of your favorite trinkets, old notes, and photos. Or fill it with wise sayings, fortunes, and candy to share with friends. There's no end to the list of ways you can use a box like this. Simply choose a theme, decorate, and fill your box with something special and fun.

What You Need

Empty matchbox

Acrylic paint, 3-D paint, or markers

Paintbrush

Scraps of colored paper

Scissors

Glue

Sequins, fake gemstones, charms, stickers (optional)

Photos, notes, fortunes, and treasures (optional)

What You Do

1. Paint the inside of the matchbox drawer, or cut a piece of paper and glue it in place.

2. Brush a little glue onto the box and cover it with layers of colored paper. You could also paint the box. Use glue to add decorations, such as beads, sequins, charms, or anything else that inspires you. Make a collage on the box by gluing cut-out magazine images in place, and spreading a thin layer of decoupage glue over the design to protect it (see page 9).

3. Fill the box with your favorite treasures and open it when you need a little inspiration.

THE "I CAN'T BELIEVE I ATE PIZZA OUT OF THIS BOX LAST NIGHT" BOX

After you've stuffed yourself with all the pizza your stomach can handle, turn the cardboard box that kept the pizza warm into a cool vanity case or collector's box.

What You Need

Pizza box

Acrylic paints or colored markers

Paintbrush

Ruler

Pencil

Cardboard

Scissors

Hot glue gun and glue sticks

Mirror

Assorted baubles, glass beads, buttons, sequins, or other objects

Water-based sealer

What You Do

1. Paint the inside of the pizza box and let it dry.

2. Decide what you want to keep in the pizza box, then draw outlines for individual compartments inside the bottom of the box. Measure the objects you want to keep in the box to figure out how large or small to make the compartments.

3. Measure and cut the cardboard into pieces to fit along the lines you just drew, then decorate the pieces with paint or markers. Let the paint or ink dry.

4. Starting in one corner of the box, glue the cardboard pieces in place one at a time. For each piece of cardboard, squeeze a bead of hot glue along one edge, then press the edge in place inside the box (figure 1).

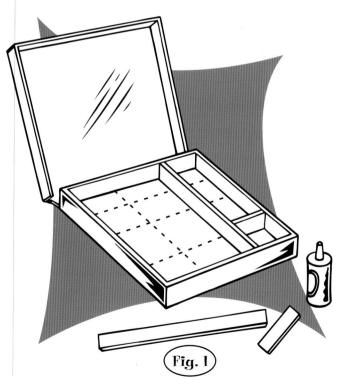

Fig. 1

5. Use the ruler and pencil to measure the area inside the pizza box lid for the mirror. You can buy a precut mirror at a craft store or home supply store.

6. Drizzle hot glue on the back of the mirror and press it in place on the box lid. Decorate the rest of the box with paint, and hot glue fake gemstones, glass beads, and other objects to the box.

7. To keep the lid open, prop the box against a wall, or make a stand by hot gluing a long piece of thick cardboard to the top of the box. Bend the bottom of the cardboard to make a foot to prop against a tabletop (figure 2).

8. Protect all of your hard work by brushing a layer of water-based sealer over the box, inside and out. When the coating is dry, fill your new and improved pizza box with your favorite things.

Fig. 2

Did Ya Know?

Pizza may well be your favorite food (in the USA alone, 350 slices of pizza are eaten each second!), but did you know that its popularity spans the globe? Depending on where you live, you can get pizza topped with pepperoni, mayonnaise, pineapple, red herring, green peas, coconut, and even squid ink. Ummm...please hold the squid ink.

HANDY HOLDER
PICTURE FRAME

This handy frame keeps all your hair accessories organized and saves you time when every second counts. Hang it near your mirror and decorate it with all those old, broken butterfly clips and barrettes you just hate to throw away.

What You Need

Photograph

Ruler

Piece of corrugated cardboard, 9 x 11 inches (22.9 x 27.9 cm)

Pencil

Craft knife

Piece of smooth cardboard, 10 x 12 inches (25.4 x 30.5 cm)

Craft glue or rubber cement

White paper and pencil

Scissors

Felt squares in bright green, dark green, light pink, and dark pink

1 orange pipe cleaner

Broken hair accessories to match your design (butterflies, dragonflies, flowers, etc.)

Piece of ribbon long enough to hang your finished frame

What You Do

1. Use the ruler to help you center the photograph on the smooth side of the corrugated cardboard, and outline the edges of the photo onto the cardboard with a pencil.

2. To make the frame for the photo, use the craft knife to cut around the inside of the box you just drew. Remember to place an extra piece of cardboard under the project, so you don't cut the surface you're working on with the craft knife.

3. Glue the photo in the center of the 10 x 12-inch (25.4 x 30.5 cm) piece of cardboard. Spread glue on the back of the corrugated cardboard frame, center it around the photo, and press it against the base (figure 1).

Fig. 1

4. Trace the flower template (below, right) onto white paper, and cut out the flower parts to use as stencils for drawing leaves on the bright green felt and flower blossoms on the pink pieces of felt.

5. Cut out the flowers and leaves, then cut two long strips from the dark green felt to make flower stems.

6. Arrange the flowers, leaves, and stems on the frame, and mark on the felt where the stems cross over the hole in the frame. Cut the stems at the marks, and put the top and bottom halves of the stems back in place on the frame. Glue the felt to the cardboard frame.

7. Cut the pipe cleaner in four pieces. Curl one end of each piece, and glue the straight ends inside the flower blossoms as seen in the project photo.

8. Glue your assortment of broken hair clips to the cardboard for decoration.

9. When the hair clips have dried to the cardboard, flip over the frame and glue the ends of the ribbon to the back of the frame, ½ inch (1.3 cm) from the sides and ½ inch (1.3 cm) from the top edge. Let the glue dry before hanging your frame.

10. Clip your good hair accessories around the frame and to the ridges in the corrugated cardboard.

PICTURE PERFECT PHOTO ALBUM

Photos are even more fun to share with friends when they're organized in photo albums, and your favorite pictures will last longer, too. The recycled paper pages in this album give you space to write comments next to your favorite snapshots, and the cardboard covers will keep it all together even while traveling in your overstuffed backpack.

What You Need

2 pieces of cardboard, each 5 x 7 inches (12.7 x 17.8 cm)*

Stamps and ink or paint

Thick paper

Ruler

Pencil

Scissors

Hole punch or nail

Yarn, string, lanyard, or wire

Self-adhesive photo mounts

3 x 5-inch (7.6 x 12.7 cm) or smaller photographs*

* You can alter this design to hold larger photographs by making the cardboard and album pages a little larger than the photos.

What You Do

1. Use stamps and different colors of ink to print designs on both pieces of cardboard. You could also decorate the cardboard with paints or markers. Set the cardboard covers aside.

2. Decide the number of pages you want in your photo album. Cut the paper into 5 x 7-inch (12.7 x 17.8 cm) rectangles to make the album pages.

3. Measure 1 inch (2.5 cm) from the left edge of each piece of cardboard and mark a hole at 1 inch (2.5 cm), 2½ inches (6.4 cm), and 4 inches (10.2 cm) from the top edge of the cardboard.

4. Use the hole punch or nail to make a hole through the cardboard at each mark (figure 1). Stack the paper and punch holes in the same spots so they line up with the holes in the cardboard.

5. Thread a piece of the yarn (string, lanyard, or wire) through each set of holes in the covers and through all the pages in between. Tie the ends of each piece of yarn together, but not too tightly, or the book will be difficult to open (figure 2).

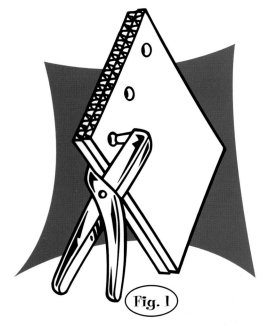

Fig. 1

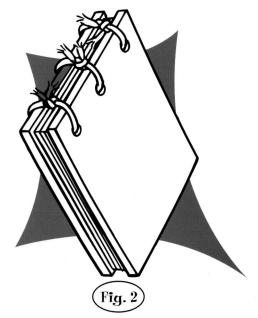

Fig. 2

6. Place the photo mounts onto each of the corners of your first photograph. Center the photo on a page in the album and press firmly to the paper. Repeat for the rest of your photos until your album is full (figure 3).

Fig. 3

Did Ya Know?

You can easily make your own stamps by cutting shapes out of one piece of cardboard and gluing them in a pattern on a second piece of cardboard. Or, follow the directions for making stamps from polystyrene trays on pages 32-34.

TROUBLE AT SEA

Shipwrecks, mermaids, whales, sharks, pirates, and coral reefs are the fascinating subjects of some of the best books and movies ever created. But when it comes right down to it, we landlubbers have a funny way of showing our appreciation for the sea. For decades, the ocean has served as a big garbage dump for ships of all kinds, while beach goers have left their picnic lunches to wash out with the tide.

Every day, huge nets catch the ocean's creatures, oil spills blacken its surface, and pollution pours into it from the rivers that drain every continent. People used to believe that the sea was so vast and deep (after all it covers two-thirds of the planet), it could absorb anything thrown into it. Now we're realizing that even the sea has limits.

During a recent International Coastal Cleanup, organized by The Ocean Conservancy, volunteers from at least 100 countries scoured the beaches and collected more than 13 million pounds (5 million kg) of trash! They also found thousands of animals, from sea turtles to birds, entangled in plastic six-pack rings, fishing gear, and plastic bags. In fact, plastic seems to be the most abundant type of ocean debris, and since it takes so long to decompose, it just keeps piling up.

Even if you live far from the ocean, some of your trash eventually makes its way to sea after a long journey down sewer pipes, streams, and rivers. Do your part to clean up and protect the world's oceans. Carefully dispose of chemicals and paints, help with a stream or beach cleanup, eat only fish that is not overharvested, and learn about the problems that plague our marine cousins. Visit an aquarium for an up-close

view of the amazing creatures that depend on a healthy ocean for survival, and visit your local library for books that will take you on underwater adventures.

Salvaged Seat

The ugliest piece of furniture you've ever seen may be taking up space in your basement, garage, attic, or bedroom. What on Earth are you going to do with it?

A. Throw it away so it can join the growing heap of trash at your local dump.

B. Sell it at a yard sale since there's bound to be someone who'll want it.

C. Give it a makeover using old magazines, glue, and paint, and turn it into an object you'll want to use all of the time.

If you picked C, read on; if you chose B, see what else you have for sale; and if you picked A, go back to the beginning of this book!

What You Need

Old bench or any piece of old furniture

Dust mask

Gloves

100-grit sandpaper

Rag

White acrylic paint or housepaint (optional)

Paintbrushes, one large and one small

Old magazines and photographs

Scissors

Acrylic paint

Newspapers

Old kitchen sponge

Tape (optional)

Decoupage glue (see page 9)

Clear acrylic spray enamel or water-based sealer

What You Do

1. If you like the color of the furniture, and the paint is in good condition, leave it as is. If the paint is chipping, ask an adult to help you sand the bench with the sandpaper and wipe it with the rag to remove any dirt and loose paint. Wear the dusk mask and gloves so you won't breathe in or absorb the dust and paint.

2. Cut pictures from old magazines, and trim photos to make a scene to cover the bench. If you have a theme for the bench, such as our ocean theme, choose a paint color that complements the theme.

3. Paint the bench with the acrylic paint color of your choice, and let it dry. For this bench, we painted the whole thing green and used the sponge to dab a thin layer of blue paint along the sides and legs of the bench.

4. Arrange all of your pictures on the top of the bench (or tape them to the sides of the legs) to make a collage of overlapping images.

5. Use the small paintbrush to spread a thin layer of decoupage glue on the backs of all of the pictures on the top of your collage. Stick the pictures back in place over the bottom layer of pictures.

6. For this step, work in small sections to keep your collage together. Lift up part of your collage at one corner and spread a layer of the decoupage glue on the bench with the larger paintbrush. Press the collage of pictures back in place. Repeat across the bench until all of the pictures have been glued down. If any of the pictures hang over the edge of the bench, trim them with the scissors.

7. When the collage is finished, spread a layer of decoupage glue over the surface of the collage to seal and protect the design. The glue will look cloudy but will dry clear.

8. Take your new and improved bench outside, set it on the newspapers, and spray the whole thing with the acrylic enamel, or coat it with water-based sealer, to protect the design and prepare the bench for use.

SAFETY TIP: Old furniture and building materials may have been painted with lead paint, which is dangerous for people, especially kids, to breathe in or to eat. Ask an adult to contact someone who can determine whether or not a piece of furniture has been painted with lead paint. Don't sand a piece of furniture you may suspect has been painted with lead paint.

RECYCLED RAIN STICK

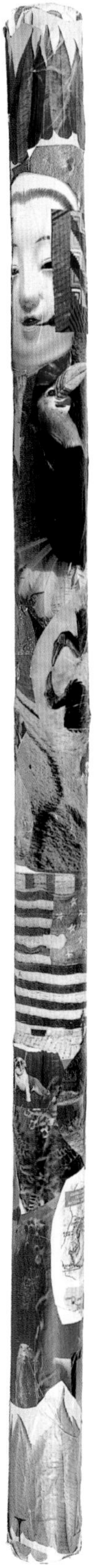

Rain sticks are traditionally made from dead cactuses. The thorns of the cactus are pushed inside of the hollow cactus stick and pebbles are poured into the cactus. When the cactus stick is turned upside down, the pebbles rattle down the stick and bounce off the thorns, mimicking the sweet sound of rain. Here's how you can make your own version of a rain stick—minus the cactus and desert—with an old mailing tube, nails, and a handful of beans.

What You Need

Thick cardboard tube (mailing tube with caps, carpet roll, or wrapping paper roll)

Several nails, as long as the width of the tube*

Hammer

Glue

Thick paper, paper bag, or newspaper

Packing tape

Handful of dried beans

Magazines

Scissors

Decoupage glue (see page 9)

Paintbrush

* You can also use toothpicks, long matchsticks, or pieces of a wire coat hanger that are as long as the width of the tube.

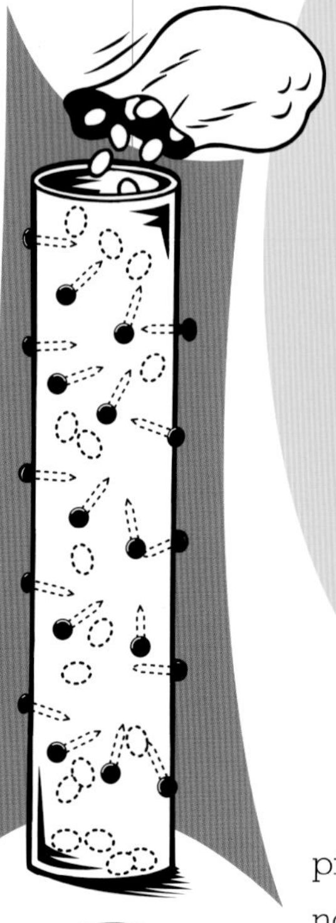

What You Do

1. Hammer the nails down the length of the tube in such a way that they make a spiral pattern (figure 1). These are called the *baffles*. If you're using short pieces of wire or toothpicks as the baffles, use a nail to make holes in the tube, then stick the wire pieces or toothpicks through the holes. Put a

Fig. 1

little glue in the holes to help hold the baffles in place. Set the tube aside until the glue is dry.

2. Cover one end of the tube with thick paper and tape (or use a cap if you have one).

3. Pour the dried beans into the tube. Hammer more nails into the tube if you want to hear more rattling.

Did Ya Know?

At the base of the Andes Mountains in South America lies the Atacama Desert, the driest place on Earth. Inhabitants of the region have traditionally made rain sticks from dead cactuses to use in ceremonies to pray for rain and thank the spirits for water.

4. Cover the open end of the tube with thick paper and tape (or use a cap).

5. Cut out pictures from magazines or use old photographs, colored paper, or fabric to cover the tube. Glue several layers of the pictures or paper to the tube to make sure the ends of the baffles don't poke through.

6. When you've covered the rain stick, use a paintbrush to spread a coat of decoupage glue over the collage to seal it and protect it from wear and tear.

Composting: Nature's Way to Recycle

After trash that can be recycled, food scraps make up most of the garbage that's left in your trash can. But you can recycle those scraps into compost to feed your yard, garden, and houseplants. You could even start a compost bin at your school. Not only is it Earth friendly, but your school will save money by composting cafeteria waste and using it to feed green soccer and football fields instead of buying fertilizer.

It's easy to compost, and any garden center can help you get started with a ready-made bin that fits in your backyard. Just follow these basic guidelines for helping nature recycle your food scraps.

1. Know what to compost. Usually, it's best to keep meat and dairy products out of your compost bin, but fruits and vegetables (and their peel), grains, stale cookies, eggshells, shredded paper, plant clippings, and leaves break down quickly in a proper bin. You can also turn old pet cage liners, such as wood shavings and alfalfa, as well as cotton from fish-tank filters, into your compost.

2. Keep a small bin with a tight-fitting lid in your kitchen for convenient collection of food scraps, and when it's full, empty it into your outdoor bin. Shred larger materials before adding them to the pile for quicker results.

3. Just like you, the tiny organisms that feed on your compost pile can't survive on bread alone. Most of what you put in your compost bin is either green or brown, and you need a little more brown stuff than green. The green matter is made up of nitrogen-rich plant scraps, fruits, vegetables, and grass clippings. The brown matter is carbon-rich stuff including wood shavings, egg cartons, and yard waste. Bacteria and fungi are the first organisms to go to work on your compost, breaking it down into food for themselves as well as the earthworms, beetles, and centipedes that will join them in the compost pile. A compost pile with a good mixture of materials provides the right amount of food to all the tiny organisms living in it.

4. Like all living creatures, the waste eaters in your compost pile need oxygen. Turn your pile with a shovel or rake at least once a week to get fresh air into the mix. Turning the pile will also help break up clumps of materials so they'll decompose faster. While you're turning it, spray a little water on the pile to keep the materials moist.

5. You can even add worms to your compost bin if you live in a moderate climate where temperatures stay between 50° and 70° F (17° and 21° C) throughout most of the year.

WASTE-MUNCHING WORMS

Go outside, find a patch of grass, put your ear to the ground, and listen. Hear anything? If you live in Korumburra, Australia, home of the world's longest earthworm, you might hear the sucking and slurping sounds of a 3-foot-long (1 meter) *Megascolides australis* as it tunnels through the ground. That's one giant worm!

You probably don't have any worms that big in your backyard, but you should find a few of the finger-length variety managing nature's soil factory out there.

Underground and in compost piles, bacteria and other microorganisms help worms digest nutrients from dead plants and animals. Worm slime contains the nitrogen that plants use as food, and worm tunnels allow air to circulate through soil, providing space for young plants to spread their roots. Like compost, *worm castings* (the technical term for worm poop) add valuable nutrients to plants, and some people use specially designed worm composters to break down their food scraps.

Redworms are the hungriest type of earthworm. They'll eat just about anything, from telephone directories to food garbage, and can eat up to half their body weight daily. That's equal to the average kid in your school eating 40 to 50 pounds (18 to 23 kg) of food every day! So the next time you get in trouble for slipping your leftovers to the dog, ask for a compost bin and a bag of worms to feed.

WORM MATH

1 pound (.45 kg) worms + ½ pound (.23 kg) paper & food garbage = 100 percent compost for feeding plants

NEWSPAPER SHELF

Newspapers can take decades to decompose once they get buried in landfills; in fact, archaeologists have found newspapers that were still readable in landfills from 40 years ago! Instead of letting them hang around the dump, roll your newspapers into a surprisingly strong shelf, and hang it in your closet or anyplace you need some extra space.

What You Need

112 full sheets of newspaper (approximately one weekend's worth of newspapers)

Tape

Acrylic paint and paintbrush

Water-based sealer

Thin nail, 2 inches (5 cm) long

Medium gauge wire*

Nail clipper or scissors

Buttons or beads (optional)

*Telephone wire, stereo cable, and old coathangers are also perfect to use for hanging your shelf.

What You Do

1. Layer 14 sheets of newspaper, one on top of the other.

2. Starting at one end, tightly roll the stack of papers (photo 1). Tape the roll at each end and in the center to hold it together (photo 2).

3. With 14 more sheets, make another roll of newspapers, then tape the two rolls together at each end and in the center.

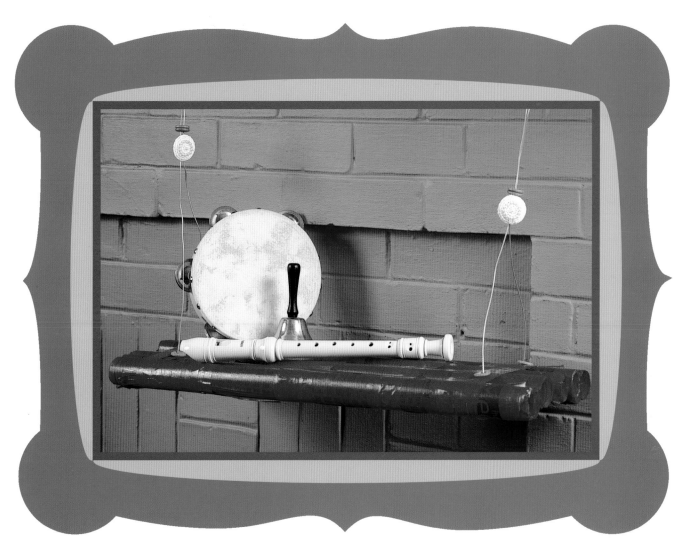

(photo 3). Continue to make rolls, taping them in pairs, until you have four pairs of rolls (8 rolls all together).

4. Now use the tape to bind two pairs of rolls together to make a flat of four (photo 4 on page 106). Make a second flat of four.

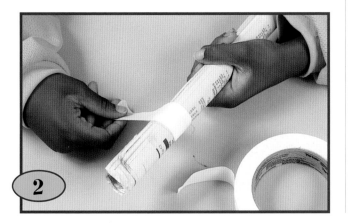

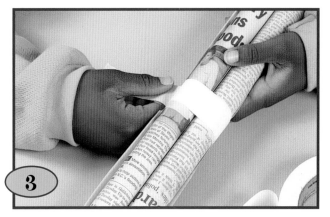

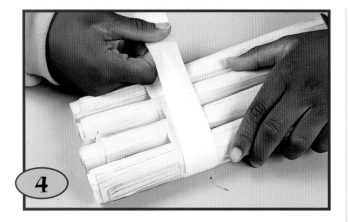

4

5

5. Bind both flats together to make the shelf. Wrap the tape around all the rolls at each end and in the center (photo 5).

6. Paint the entire shelf with the acrylic paint and let it dry.

7. Use a clean paintbrush to spread a layer of the water-based sealer all over the shelf to seal and protect it from wear and tear.

8. Use the nail to make two holes at each end of the shelf between the second and third newspaper rolls and the sixth and seventh newspaper rolls.

9. Run a piece of wire through the sets of holes at each end of the shelf to make

hangers (photo 6). Decide where you're going to put your shelf, and cut the ends of the wire as long as you need them for hanging.

10. If you want, slip buttons or beads down the wires on each side of the shelf for decoration. Twist the wires together below and above the buttons or beads to hold them in place. Twist the loose ends of the wire together, and your shelf is ready for hanging.

Here's an idea: Instead of painting the shelf, make the shelf rolls from the comics section of the newspaper, then spread the water-based sealer over the shelf for protection.

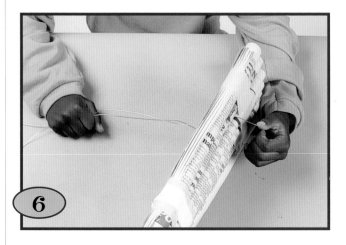

6

Did Ya Know?

The typical print run for a paper-packed, Sunday edition of a national newspaper requires an amount of wood fiber equal to nearly 75,000 trees!

Odds & Ends
Scrap Fabric Message Board

Here's a message board you can really empty your pockets onto. Clip old clothespins around the edges of the board to hold photos, and hang a roll of register tape on one side for writing down reminders. Stash notes and a pen in the pocket, and pin homework assignments to the board. The best part is, you can cover the board with that favorite old shirt, pair of jeans, or bandanna you haven't worn in years but keep holding onto no matter how many times you clean out your closet.

What You Need

2 large cardboard boxes, 16 x 20 inches (40.6 x 50.8 cm) or larger

Ruler and pencil

Scissors

Newspapers

Watered down wood glue (1 part glue to 3 parts water)

Kitchen sponge or paintbrush

Heavy books

Scraps of fabric or one large piece to cover the board

Pocket from an old pair of pants or an old shirt

Brass fasteners or upholstery tacks

Clothespins

String

Pushpins or thumbtacks

Cord or ribbon

Screwdriver (optional)

What You Do

1. Use the ruler and pencil to draw four 16 x 20 inch (40.6 x 50.8 cm) rectangles on the sides of the cardboard boxes. Cut the rectangles from the boxes.

2. Lay out the newspapers on the floor in an out-of-the-way space. Stack the pieces of cardboard on the newspapers. Spread the wood glue with the sponge or paintbrush between each layer of cardboard to stick them together. Set heavy books on top of the cardboard stack so it'll stay pressed together. Let the glue dry overnight.

3. Use one large piece of fabric, make a collage from fabric scraps, or use some combination to cover the board. Spread the wood glue on one side of the board, then press the fabric in place with your hands. Start in the center of the board, and smooth the fabric out to the sides. Fold extra fabric over the edges of the board and spread a little glue under it to hold it in place.

4. Spread a thin layer of glue on top of the fabric, and use the sponge to push the glue through the fibers to the cardboard. This layer of glue will stiffen the fabric so it will last longer. When dry, cover the other side of the board with glue and fabric.

5. Tie the cord or ribbon tightly around the width of the board, near the top. Clip a clothespin over the cord on each side of the board to hold it in place (figure 1). As an alternative, punch a hole in each of the top cor-

ners of the board with the screwdriver. Slip one end of the cord through each of the holes, and tie knots in the ends to keep the cord from slipping out of the board. Use the cord to hang your new message board from a nail or hook in your room.

Decorate Your Message Board

Attach the pocket to the board with brass fasteners or upholstery tacks. Clip clothespins around the edges of your board to use as note and picture holders. You can even use them to hold mini organizers, such as the baskets shown on the board on page 107. Cut a piece of string as wide as the top of your message board, tie a knot at each end of the string, and hook the string between the clothespins across the top of the board. Clip mini-clothespins to the string for more handy holders. Stick pushpins or thumbtacks in a corner of the board, and hang the roll of register tape from a loop of rope hooked onto one of the clothespins.

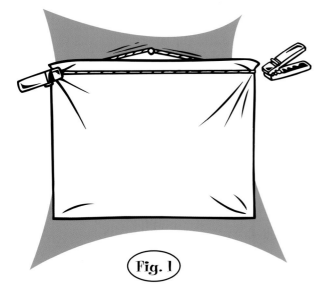

Fig. 1

GLASS
goodies

Glass helps us explore and examine the microscopic cells in our bodies, our own reflection, the world that surrounds us, and the stars in space. Without it, we may have never invented binoculars, microscopes, magnifying lenses, eyeglasses, lightbulbs, telescopes, televisions, cameras, kaleidoscopes, and mirrors there goes science class and most of the discoveries and inventions of the last thousand years. The first people to make glass from mixing sand, wood ash, and lime in a really, really hot fire never could have imagined how their discovery would change the world.

Nowadays, grocery store aisles are stocked with glass containers, and your kitchen cupboards are probably filled with glasses, bottles, and jars. Most of those food containers are made from recycled or reused glass. In fact, bottle glass is 100 percent reusable! Isn't it odd then, that it still ends up in trash cans destined for landfills and incinerators? If you live in a community that charges a deposit on glass containers, you

know the cash advantage of redeeming your glass. All those containers you return for money are cleaned and refilled with food or drink and restocked on store shelves. In fact, the average bottle can be reused 20 times. Glass containers that can't be refilled are recycled—old glass is melted down and molded into new forms. Even though recycling glass still requires a lot of energy (remember the really, really hot fire?), ultimately it saves resources and reduces the load that ends up in landfills.

If you don't have a deposit program where you live, talk to your parents about getting one started. Meanwhile, we'll show you lots of ways to reuse glass and mirror. Just turn the page to find out how to make a garden border by burying bottles in your yard, turn large jars into mini-greenhouses, and make a snow globe out of a pickle jar! With an adult's help and some colorful paints, you'll even transform broken mirrors into good-luck gifts. And since we're on the subject of things that break, we'll show you how to turn the shattered pieces of your mom's favorite vase or dish into a gift that'll make her smile. After all, clay pottery, porcelain, and china are practically cousins of glass. Best of all, you'll learn new ways to decorate old jars and bottles to make cool, reusable containers for everyone in your home.

CRAFTS FOR KIDS

LUAU SNOW GLOBE

You can make it snow in Hawaii!
And you don't have to have a wizard's
powers, just an old glass
jar, glycerin, water, and
glitter. Not into hula
girls? No matter.
Imagine the scene
you want to
create...maybe it's a
rocket blasting into
starry space or fish
floating in a sparkling
sea. Scour through the
boxes of old toys in the
attic for inspiration, and
in a few easy steps you
can make a snow globe
of your own.

What You Need

One clean, 16-ounce (480 mL) glass jar with a screw-on lid (pickle jars work great!)

Plastic figures and toys that fit inside the jar

Silicone adhesive *

Sand or small pebbles (optional)

2 ounces (60 mL) of glycerin (available at craft stores)

Liquid measuring cup

14 ounces (420 mL) of water

Eyedropper

Glitter

Teaspoon

* Silicone adhesive is needed only if you want to permanently hold the objects you've chosen in place in the jar.

What You Do

1. To make a scene like ours, set the jar lid upside down and arrange your figurines in place on the inside of the lid. Make sure the glass jar will fit over your scene once the cap is completely screwed on.

2. Squeeze some of the silicone adhesive onto the jar lid and stick the plastic figures in the goo. While the silicone adhesive is still sticky, you can sprinkle sand, glitter, or pebbles over it to cover the inside of the lid for your scene. Let the lid sit overnight so the adhesive has time to dry before going on to step 3.

3. Check to see if the silicone adhesive feels firm when you push on it with a pencil. If the pencil goes through it, you need to let the silicone adhesive sit longer. If it's firm, you're ready to assemble the snow globe.

4. Move all of your materials to a sink, and fill the jar with water and the glycerin.

5. Add a teaspoon of glitter to the jar for the "snow," then make sure the jar is completely filled with water so there won't be any air bubbles in your snow globe.

6. Time to cap your jar. Guide the tops of the figures on the jar lid through the mouth of the jar and into the water mixture. Some water will spill out. Screw the lid on evenly and tightly. Voila! Your snow globe is complete.

Here's an idea: Follow the steps above, but choose objects that would look cool floating freely in the jar, such as mini-plastic fish, and leave out the silicone adhesive.

Tip: Add two or three drops of household bleach to the water to prevent mold and cloudiness from building up over time.

TERRIFIC TERRARIUMS

Turn large glass or plastic bottles into terrariums or miniature biospheres—the glass or plastic holds water, gases, and nutrients inside the container in balance with the plants that live in them. Your school's cafeteria and restaurants are great sources for large food jars and so is the bulk food aisle at grocery stores. Once you set up your terrarium, it will take care of itself (except for needing a spritz of water now and then).

What You Need

Clean, clear, large glass or plastic jar with lid (make sure your hand fits in the jar)

Small stones and pebbles

Soil

Spoon

Small green plants, especially moss, ivy, and ferns

Bark

Scrap piece of wood

Hammer and nail

Spray bottle of water

Note: For a desert terrarium, substitute sand for soil and cactuses for the green plants.

What You Do

1. Cover the bottom of the jar with the small stones and pebbles.

2. Scoop the soil into the jar until the bottom third of the jar is filled.

3. Set your plants into the soil so the roots are covered. Scoop more soil into the jar around the plants to support them. Finish the arrangement by placing the bark and moss on top of the soil and around the plants.

4. Set the jar lid on the scrap piece of wood and punch holes in it with the hammer and nail.

5. Mist the plants in your new terrarium with the spray bottle of water, then cap the jar with the lid. (Notice how water vapor forms on the sides of the jar.) Keep your jar in a partly sunny spot and spray with water whenever the sides of the jar look dry.

CREATIVE WAYS TO TAKE OUT THE TRASH

Create the coolest, Earth-friendliest yard on the block with bottles, egg cartons, old shoes, and more. Not only will your neighbors do a double take when they realize those are corks serving as mulch in your mom's flowerbed, but they'll also be inspired to take a closer look in their garbage cans for reusable items.

Plant a row of bottles, upside down and side by side, to make a border that will glisten in the sun and reflect moonbeams at night. Collect soda, water, and juice bottles, and ask your parents to save their wine bottles. Remove the labels from the bottles. Dig a trench deep enough to cover the necks of the bottles, set the bottles in the trench, and pack the soil around them to keep them upright.

Your old, stinky shoes will smell as good as roses when you turn them into planters. Fill the shoes with potting soil, plant some seeds or young plants in them, and set them in a sunny spot.

Cardboard egg cartons make perfect seed starters, and since they're biodegradable, they'll break down naturally to become part of the soil. Bury seeds under potting soil in each of the compartments in the egg carton. When the seedlings are large enough to plant, tear the carton into single sections and set each section with its seedling in a larger pot of soil or in the ground in your garden.

Transform that plastic, kiddie pool that's still behind the garage into a mini-pond to provide a home for frogs or fish. Hide a water pump in a stack of rocks in the center of the pool for a simple fountain. Ask the staff at a garden center, home improvement store, or pet store for advice and supplies to get started. With the right mix of plants and animals, your pond will mostly take care of itself.

BETTER-THAN-A-BROKEN-DISH TRAY

Accidents happen, but the next time you break one of your mom's favorite plates, you don't have to throw it away or hide the pieces. Instead, decorate an old tray with those trash-bound pieces to use for making your mom breakfast in bed. She's certain to love your thoughtfulness and forgive your clumsiness.

What You Need

Gloves

Pieces from broken dishes or tile (flat pieces work best)

Small broom and dustpan

Thick plastic bag

Towel

Hammer

Tumbler (see page 10)

Wooden serving tray*

Rag

White acrylic paint

Acrylic paint to match one of the colors of the shards

Paintbrush

Adhesive shelf paper**

Scissors

Craft glue

Newspapers

Clear acrylic spray enamel

* You can buy a plain wooden tray at a craft store.

** This is the sticky, plastic-coated paper used to cover shelves and line the insides of drawers. You can find it at grocery, home improvement, and craft stores.

Did Ya Know?

Even though a lot of glass is collected for recycling, Americans alone throw away enough glass to fill the world's tallest building—the Petronas Twin Towers in Malaysia—every two weeks!

What You Do

1. Wear gloves to collect the broken pieces in the dustpan, then pour them into the thick plastic bag. Fold the towel around the bag so there aren't any gaps, and set both on the floor. Smash the towel with the hammer a couple of times to break the pieces inside it into even smaller pieces.

2. Pour the smaller pieces into the tumbler, and follow the manufacturer's instructions to smooth the sharp edges of the pieces.

3. Wipe the tray with a damp rag to get rid of any dirt and dust.

4. If the tray has old paint on it, first cover it with a coat of white acrylic paint and let dry. Paint the tray with the colored acrylic paint.

5. When the tray is dry and the pieces in the tumbler are smooth, spread them on a table next to your tray. Move the tumbled pieces around inside the tray until you've created a design or pattern you like and the tray's surface is covered. Like a jigsaw puzzle, you may have to take some pieces out and move others around to fill in the gaps.

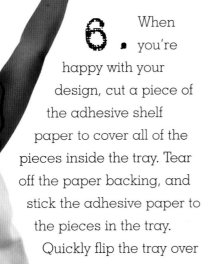

6. When you're happy with your design, cut a piece of the adhesive shelf paper to cover all of the pieces inside the tray. Tear off the paper backing, and stick the adhesive paper to the pieces in the tray. Quickly flip the tray over onto the table so the sticky paper and the design come out.

7. Spread the glue inside the bottom of the tray. Then quickly flip the adhesive paper and the shards back into the tray. Press the paper and pieces into the tray so the pieces set in the glue, then let sit for a couple of hours.

8. When the glue has dried and the pieces are stuck to the tray, remove the adhesive paper. Set the tray on top of the newspapers, outside, and spray the whole thing with clear acrylic enamel. The enamel will help seal the design and bring out the colors in the pieces. Once the enamel dries, your new tray will be ready for use.

Think Locally: Take Action to Make Your House Earth Friendly

If your parents are like most these days, they're stretched between work, shuttling you around to activities, cleaning, cooking, shopping, paying bills, and somehow squeezing in their own hobbies and friends. It's all they can do to even remember to take out the trash and recyclables. So instead of lecturing them about the state of the world's environment, help them take action by turning your house into an Earth-friendly home with these simple, time- and money-saving ideas.

1: The average dump is 26-percent organic waste, which includes bags of leaves, branches, and food waste. So start composting and turn food scraps into usable soil for a garden or indoor plants. Place a decorated container with a tight-fitting lid in a convenient place (like near the kitchen sink) to hold all your family's leftover food, banana peels, tea bags, and coffee grounds until you have time to dump the scraps in an outdoor bin.

2: Let's face it, when people don't recycle, it's often out of laziness or what they see as inconvenience. Keep a copy of your city's recycling schedule and the list of acceptable items on your refrigerator for easy reference. Keep a long-handled scrub brush near the sink for rinsing and cleaning recyclable food containers. If you don't have an official recycling bin, use a label to designate a box, bucket, or extra trash can for holding recyclables, and keep it near your kitchen garbage.

3: Go shopping and help choose family-size containers and bulk food items to cut down on waste-producing packaging, save money, and reduce trips to the grocery store. Reuse perfectly good glass and plastic food containers to store bulk foods and to divide large portions into smaller servings. Watch for other containers you can't recycle, and save them for other creative uses around the house.

4: Plastic bags are handy and convenient but after one use they usually get

tossed in the garbage can. Wash used plastic bags, then turn them inside out and clip them to a mini-clothesline in your kitchen so you can reuse them.

5: Use rags instead of tree-gobbling paper towels. Rags are washable, reusable, and tough—especially, when it comes to rubbing goop off of countertops and scrubbing stains out of carpets. Help your parents find cleansers that say "biodegradable" and "phosphate-free" on their labels. White vinegar diluted with water makes a strong, natural cleanser that works on lots of surfaces from windows to floors. It's great for cleaning pet cages, too, because it's safe and hides odors. After cleaning with the vinegar, rinse the surface with water or a wet rag.

MORE TIPS:

Use cloth or mesh bags for groceries and keep them in the trunk of the family car so they'll be there for every trip to the store. If you forget your bags, ask a store clerk for one of their newly emptied packing boxes to carry your items home in. When all else fails and the clerk asks, "Paper or plastic?" choose the one that you'll reuse or recycle most easily.

Stuff plastic grocery bags in one of the widowed socks you've kept around in hopes that the mate will miraculously appear one day. Nail the sock to a wall in a closet or cabinet in your kitchen for convenience.

Old toothbrushes are great mini-scrubbers for hard-to-reach spots and narrow containers.

ADULT ASSISTANCE NECESSARY

ODDS & ENDS

Wrinkled Wax Batiks

Batik is an ancient technique from India that uses melted wax and dyes to make designs and patterns on fabric. You can do simple batik in your kitchen by melting the wax from broken crayons and burned-down candles to decorate old sheets. Dip the sheets in fabric dye to create unusual bedding, curtains, and tapestries for your room. You can even use batik to make your own designs on T-shirts.

What You Need

- Scrap paper and colored pencils, crayons, or markers
- Broken crayons and old candles
- Coffee can
- Large cooking pot
- Use of a stove
- Old cotton sheet and pillowcase
- Newspapers or paper bags
- Assorted paintbrushes
- Plastic gloves
- Red, orange, yellow, and blue fabric dye
- Salt
- 4 quart-size (liter) jars
- Old spoon
- Hair dryer
- Tub
- Old stiff brush
- Paper bags
- Iron and ironing board
- 2 yards (1.8 meters) of gold fringe
- Hot glue gun and glue sticks

What You Do

1. **Please Read Me!** This project involves boiling water, hot wax, colored dyes, and ironing, so for your safety and fun, please don't attempt this without an adult's help. Since some of these steps require you to work quickly, gather all of the

materials and spread them out on a large worktable before you start. Cover the table with newspaper or cardboard to protect its surface, and wear old clothes in case you get some dye on you. Also, remember to wear gloves while working with the fabric dyes.

2. Plan your design and decide which colors you'll need. It's a good idea to draw a sketch of your idea on a piece of paper, and color it in so you'll know where to paint the fabric dye on the sheet. Since fabric dyes expand from where you first apply them, you should keep your design simple, with clear, wide shapes so the colors won't all blend together. You'll use melted wax to outline the individual parts of your design and block the fabric from the dye in the places you want white space. Note: The wax will darken the fabric some.

3. Remove any labels from the crayons, then fill the coffee can halfway with the wax stuff—you can melt more later, so don't put any more in the can (photo 1). Put the coffee can in the large pot and fill the pot about halfway with water. Don't put water in the can with the wax.

4. With help from an adult, place the pot with the can of wax stuff in it on the stove, and bring the water to a boil. Keep an eye on the wax in the coffee can, and make sure the water in the large pot doesn't boil out. Carefully add water to the large pot as some of it boils away. Keep the heat up so the water continues to boil until all of the wax has melted (about 10 to 15 minutes).

5. When the wax has melted, ask your adult helper to move the pot over to your worktable. Lay the fabric out flat, close to the container of wax, on top of the newspaper.

6. Dip a paintbrush into the hot wax, and outline the colored areas of your design on the fabric (photo 2). Apply the wax wherever you don't want the colored dye to seep through. Let the wax dry.

7. Put on the gloves. Follow the instructions on the packages of fabric dye for mixing the dye. With most powdered, hot-water dyes, you can mix one package with a dash of salt in a quart (liter) jar of hot water. Use an old spoon or stick to stir the dye until the powder is dissolved. The more water you use, the lighter

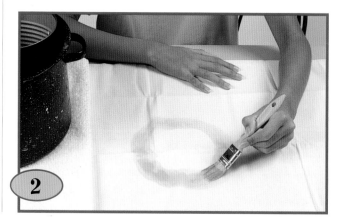

the dye will be; for really dark colors use less than a quart of water. The color will lighten as the fabric dries.

8. With a clean paintbrush, paint the colored dye on the fabric to match your design. If you want intense, dark colors you'll need to paint over the fabric several times (photo 3).

9. Use the hair dryer to dry the fabric, then wad it up into a ball so the wax crinkles and cracks.

10. Dip the fabric into a tub of cold water to rinse out some of the dye. The dye will also seep into the cracks you just made in the wax, creating cool patterns on the plain fabric beneath it. Hang the fabric to dry or use the hair dryer.

3

11. With your fingers or an old brush, scrape off as much wax from the fabric as you can. Place the fabric between sheets of newspaper or paperbags on the ironing board. Set the iron to a high setting, and slowly smooth it over the paper bags to melt the remaining wax on the fabric underneath (photo 4). The newspaper will soak up the melted wax, and later can be composted or used as mulch in a garden.

12. Line up the fringe with the bottom of the sheet or around the open end of the pillowcase, and cut it to the length you need. Then use the glue gun to spread a layer of hot glue between the fabric and the fringe, and press the materials together.

13. To finish the curtain, make a pocket at the top of the sheet to slide the curtain rod through. Lay the curtain rod across the top of the sheet and fold the fabric over the curtain rod. Use a line of hot glue across the top of the sheet, below the curtain rod, to attach the folded fabric and hold the pocket in place.

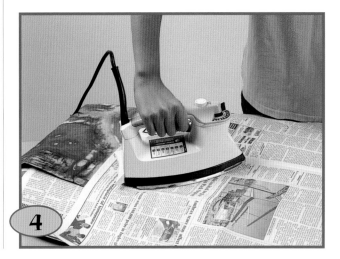
4

Good Luck Gift Mirrors

A broken mirror doesn't have to be bad luck if you decorate it with glass paints and fake lead lines to give it new life. Look for old mirrors around your house, at yard sales, or ask a glass shop for the scraps they have set aside as trash. A glass shop will also help you transform the larger pieces of a broken mirror by smoothing the sharp edges and shaping the pieces into mini-mirrors you can decorate as great, new gifts.

What You Need

Old mirror (ask for an adult's help if you want to work with a broken mirror)

Glass cleaner

Rag

1/8-inch (3 mm) fake lead line strips with adhesive backing *

Scissors

Ruler

Fine-tip permanent marker

Stained-glass paints in squeeze bottles, in citrus yellow, amber, orange, purple, and magenta

Scrap piece of cardboard to test the paints on

Cotton swabs

Toothpick, sewing needle, or pin

*Available at craft stores

What You Do

1. Clean and dry your mirror with glass cleaner and a rag.

2. Fake lead lines are strips of plastic that look like the dark lines on a stained glass window. You can use them to outline the edges of your mirror and to make patterns on the glass like the boxes on the mirror in the picture on your right. The lead lines also help keep the glass paints from running off the mirror and from mixing with the other colors in your design. To make a border, cut the lead lines into strips that are as long as each side of the mirror. Peel the paper backing off each strip and, one at a time, press each line along the matching edge of the mirror. Try to get the lead lines as close to the edges of the mirror as possible.

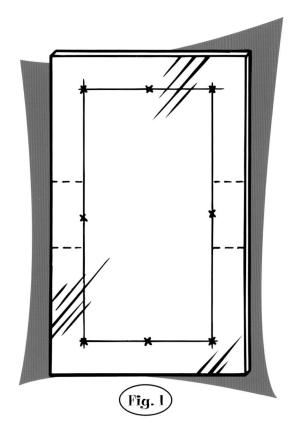

Fig. 1

3. Make the inside border by measuring 3 inches (7.6 cm) in from each edge with the ruler and marking the face of the mirror in three spots on each side with the marker. Use the ruler and marker to draw a straight line that connects all of the marks to make a box (figure 1).

4. Cut four lead lines as long as each side of the mirror and stick them to the face of the mirror along the inside border lines. Each strip should run from one edge to the opposite edge of the mirror. The lead lines will cross to make a box in each corner.

5. Cut four more lead lines, each 3 inches (7.6 cm) long. Make a box in the center of the border on each of the long sides of the mirror. Use a ruler to make sure the box lines are even and straight.

6. Paint inside each box by squeezing a base color from one of the stained-glass paint bottles until a steady line of paint comes out. (Squeeze the bottle on the piece of cardboard to get out any air bubbles in the bottle.) Move the bottle back and forth across the box until it's filled in with paint. Don't go over the lead lines with the paint, but if you do, immediately use a moist cotton swab to clean up the smudge.

7. If you're using the colors listed here, first paint with the citrus yellow using the side-to-side method, then swirl the orange paint into the box. The two colors will make a nice pattern if you don't blend them completely. Squeeze some amber-colored paint into the box over the first two colors and level with the edge of the lead lines. Use the toothpick or a pin to pop any air bubbles you see.

8. Use the same methods to paint the purple box, with purple as the base color and magenta swirled into it. You don't need to use the amber-colored paint. Paint the orange boxes with just the orange paint. Let all of the paint dry completely before handling your new and improved mirror.

GLASS JAR & BOTTLE ART

Do more than just recycle, reuse your glass containers. Sure, you could buy new containers to organize all your small stuff, but that's boring. How about transforming that perfectly good tomato sauce jar or bottle of syrup into a cool container with one or more of the five techniques featured here? Definitely not boring. Besides holding coins and trinkets, glass jars keep cookies, candy, and crackers fresh longer, so you're less likely to come back from the cupboard with a stale snack.

Wash your decorated jars and bottles by hand only; dishwashers may ruin all of your hard work. Check the labels on your paints for food safety and washing tips when it comes to using your new and improved containers.

Cosmic Colors Jar

Painting on glass is fun and pretty easy, though make sure you read the instructions on the glass paints you purchase. In some cases, you'll first have to use a surface conditioner on the jar so the paint will stick better.

What You Need

Clean glass jar with lid

Surface conditioner (required for air-dry glass paints)

1/2-inch-wide (1.3 cm), flat paintbrush

Template on page 141, or stickers

White paper and pencil

Scissors

Tape

Assorted colors of opaque glass paints, air-dry or oven bake

Pointed, round paintbrush

What You Do

1. If using air-dry glass paints, use the flat paintbrush to paint a coat of surface conditioner all over the jar, and let dry.

2. Trace the star template onto the paper with the pencil. Cut out the design and tape it to the jar to use as a stencil. Place the stickers directly on the jar to use as stencils.

3. Use the round paintbrush and one of the paint colors to outline the star shapes on the jar.

4. When the outlines are dry, remove the stickers or stencils and fill in the stars with another color of paint. Choose a third color to paint circles around the stars. Let these painted designs dry before adding more patterns to the jar.

5. Paint wavy stripes of different colors to connect the stars around the jar. Let the stripes of paint dry.

6. Decorate the stripes and circles around the stars with dots and small stars in contrasting colors of paint. Examples of contrasting colors include: red and green, orange and blue, yellow and purple.

7. Use the same color of paint you used to outline the stars in step 3 to add more star shapes around the jar and to outline some of the stripes.

8. Follow the instructions on the paint jars for baking the oven-bake paints and for washing and drying your new and improved jars.

BEAD & STAR BOTTLE

You'll need to practice with the tubes of glass outliner paints before you actually decorate your bottle, but don't worry, you'll get the hang of it quickly.

What You Need

Gold glass outliner paint (air-dry variety in tube)

Scrap piece of cardboard

Clean glass bottle with a flat area for decorating

Glass or plastic star

Small gold and blue beads

Tweezers

Newspapers

Clear acrylic spray enamel

What You Do

1. Practice using the outliner paint on the scrap piece of cardboard. Press the tip of the tube against the cardboard as you lightly squeeze the tube to get the paint flowing, then lift the tube slightly off the cardboard as you draw so the paint will leave neat, thick lines. Touch the tip of the tube against the cardboard to stop the flow of paint.

2. Now that you have the hang of it, outline the area of the bottle you want to decorate, and let the paint dry.

3. Move the tube of outliner paint back and forth, while squeezing lightly, to fill in the area inside the outline you just made.

4. Press the star shape into the paint on the jar. The wet paint should hold the star and seal it in place. Use the tweezers to set the beads in the paint around the star.

5. After all of the paint has dried, set the bottle outside on some newspapers and spray the design with the clear acrylic enamel to seal and protect it.

ETCHED GLASS BOTTLE

Etching creme is a chemical substance that can be used to make really cool designs on glass and mirrors. As with all chemicals, you need to be careful while using it. Wear gloves, ask an adult to help you, and work in a space with lots of fresh air. It may seem funny to have a material like this in an Earth-friendly book, but a little goes a long way to turn old, ordinary glass items into cool-looking containers, so we thought it was worth sharing with you. Make sure to follow the instructions on the bottle for safe cleanup and disposal.

What You Need

Clean glass bottle

Adhesive shelf paper*

Scissors

Star stickers

Rubber gloves

2 towels

Newspapers

Etching cream

Plastic spoon

Plastic scraper or a square piece of old sponge

Timer

*This is the sticky, plastic-coated paper used to cover shelves and line the insides of drawers. You can find it at home improvement, grocery, and craft stores.

What You Do

1. Cut the adhesive shelf paper into four ½-inch-wide (1.3 cm) strips the same length as the jar. Stick the strips to the jar to frame the area on the jar that you want to etch.

2. Decorate the framed-in part of the jar with the star stickers. All of the area around the stickers will look frosted after you apply the etching cream, but the glass under the stickers will remain shiny.

1

3. Make a barrier around the framed part of the jar by cutting 3-inch-wide (7.6 cm) strips of the adhesive shelf paper to stick on top of the first four strips (photo 1). These wide strips will act as wells to catch any excess etching cream that runs off of the jar when you apply it.

4. In a well-ventilated space, set the bottle on one of the towels, on top of newspapers, and out of the reach of young kids and pets. Wrap the second towel around the bottle, under the paper wells, to hold the bottle in place. Put on the rubber gloves.

5. Stir the etching cream with the spoon. Place one hand under one of the paper wells to support it, and pour some of the etching cream into the well (photo 2). Use the scraper to spread the etching cream from the well, over the bottle, and to the opposite well (photo 3). Be careful not to scrape the stickers and tear them off of the jar.

6. Follow the instructions on the etching cream bottle for the amount of time you need to let the cream set (usually 15 to 20 minutes), and start your timer. Don't touch the bottle until the time is up so the cream can work on the glass.

7. When the bottle is ready, clear the cream off of the glass and into the well you originally poured it into. (Make sure you have the gloves on.) Lift the bottle you're working on and funnel the etching cream back into its original container to reuse on another project.

8. Rinse the bottle and the scraper under running water. While water is pouring on the bottle, peel off all of the stickers and the adhesive-shelf-paper strips.

9. When you've rinsed all of the cream off the bottle, dry the bottle completely with a towel and admire the frosted design you just made.

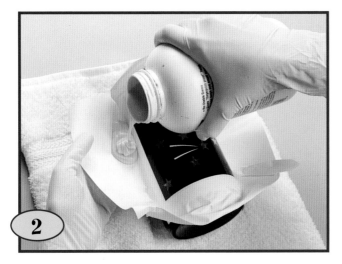

DECOUPAGE BOTTLE

It's amazing what some magazine pages and a little glue can do to spruce up old glass bottles. Once you create your first decoupage bottle, you'll be eager to make more.

What You Need

Clean glass bottle

Old magazines

Scissors

Decoupage glue (see page 9)

Paintbrush

What You Do

1. Flip through the magazines, and cut out pictures you want to use to decorate the bottle. Arrange the pictures on a table to come up with a design that you like.

2. Use the paintbrush to spread the decoupage glue around the bottle in the space you want to decorate.

3. Stick the pictures you've cut out onto the bottle in the order you arranged them. You can glue more pictures on top of the first layer until the bottle is covered with your design.

4. Spread a final coat of glue over the collage to seal and protect it. The decoupage glue will wash off in a dishwasher or if the bottle is left sitting in water, so use a damp rag to wipe the outside of the bottle when it needs cleaning. Also, use the bottle for non-food items only so you won't need to wash it all the time.

STAINED GLASS JAR

Create an authentic-looking, stained glass jar with some fake lead lines and paint. You'll marvel at how great it looks.

What You Need

Template on page 141

White paper and pencil

Scissors

Clean glass jar

Fake lead line strips with adhesive backing (available at craft stores)

Glass paints in bottles with applicator tips in red and three shades of purple

Toothpick

Crackle medium

Paintbrush

What You Do

1. Use the template as a guide for cutting the fake lead lines to the length you need to make the star and border on the bottle. Peel the paper off the fake lead lines and stick them to the bottle, copying the design in the project photo.

2. Fill in the star with the red paint, and fill the rest of the spaces around the star with the different shades of purple paint. Use the toothpick to pop any air bubbles that form in the paint.

3. When the paint on the jar is dry, cover the star with a coat of the crackle medium to finish the stained-glass look.

TRASH IN SPACE

Imagine orbiting the earth in a space station, taking photographs of the blue seas and swirling cloud patterns below, when suddenly, KABAM-KABOOM! As captain, you check your systems and your radar, but nothing registers on the screens. All seems quiet as usual out there. Your mind spins and you wonder, "Have we just entered a parallel universe? Been hit by some long-range space-gun?" You report to Mission Control on Earth, and after checking out the Space Inventory System, they inform you that you were hit by an orbiting paint flake from an old satellite. What?! Yep, believe it. Paint flakes, fuel dust from

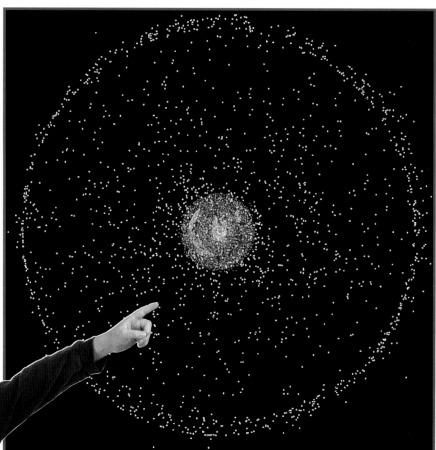

engines, and other particles smaller than your pinky fingernail can pack a big hit, especially when traveling at 17,000 miles (27,200 km) per hour. As you read this, there are millions of these mini bullets orbiting the Earth.

Orbital debris, a.k.a. "space trash," results from collisions, explosions, and natural wear and tear from the satellites and rockets that governments have been launching into space since the 1960s. The United States and The Confederation of Independent States lead the world in contributing to this orbiting space dump, followed by the European Union and Japan. The U.S. Space Surveillance Network has catalogued over 9,000 objects larger than 4 inches (10.2 cm), and estimates that there are tens of millions of smaller particles floating around Earth. All this trash has gotten the world's attention, and the United Nations is studying the problem under its Committee on the Peaceful Uses of Outer Space.

Eventually (and fortunately), most falling objects burn up as they pass through Earth's atmosphere, but on average, a hunk of trash survives the fiery journey each day, plunging into the ocean or crashing into sparsely populated areas such as Siberia, northern Canada, and the Australian Outback. While falling space junk makes for interesting stories in the remote Arctic, it presents an unwelcome challenge for astronauts who have to navigate through the growing minefield of trash that circles the Earth.

Odds & Ends

SPINNING SPACE SCULPTURE (VFR PI 2)

While scientists struggle with ways to retrieve the many pieces of space trash that orbit Earth, you can put all sorts of discarded objects together to create out-of-this-world sculpture. Scavenge your closets, garage, and basement to find dusty objects such as a bowling ball and old flashlight. Check out flea markets, thrift stores, and yard sales for an old, wooden lazy Susan to set it all in motion. Save a burned-out lightbulb to use as a moon.

With help from an adult, you'll be able to assemble all the odds and ends you've found to make your own moveable masterpiece.

What You Need

Paper and marker

Bowling ball

Wooden lazy Susan

4 finishing nails, 2 inches (5 cm) long

Hammer

3 corks

Scissors

Flashlight

Tape measure

3 feet (91.8 cm) of heavy-duty, plastic-coated electrical wire (3 or 4 conductor) *

Drill

4 screws with washers

Screwdriver

12-inch (30.5 cm) piece of coat-hanger wire

Pliers

Small rubber or plastic ball

Clear tape (optional)

Bits of colored wire, bottlecaps, knobs, and other items for decorating the flashlight

Epoxy (optional)

Acrylic paints and paintbrush

* 3 or 4 conductor electrical wire is made up of three or four individual wires bound together under a plastic coating. You'll cut the plastic coating away and separate the wires to wrap them around the flashlight. You also can wrap four pieces of coat-hanger wire together with duct tape in place of plastic coated electrical wire.

What You Do

1. Place the piece of paper over the holes in the bowling ball and mark the holes on the paper. Set the paper over the center of the lazy Susan and press the marker to the holes on the paper until the ink bleeds through, marking the lazy Susan.

2. Ask an adult to help you pound the nails into the marks you just made on the lazy Susan. The nails should go through only the top layer of the lazy Susan so it still spins. Place the bowling ball so that the ends of the nails fit into the holes. You may need to tap the nails with the hammer, bending them slightly, until they line up with the holes. Remove the bowling ball.

3. Push the corks as far into the bowling ball holes as possible (you may need to use the hammer). Trim the ends of the corks with the scissors so the bottoms of the corks are even with the surface of the bowling ball. Use the hammer and another nail to start a hole in each of the corks. Align the ends of the nails in the lazy Susan with the corked holes in the bowling ball, and push down the bowling ball against the lazy

Susan until it feels secure (figure 1). You'll have a lot of explaining to do if the bowling ball breaks free and goes soaring through the house when you give the lazy Susan a spin.

4. Choose the best-looking side of the bowling ball and mark an X on the opposite side of the lazy Susan. Remove the bowling ball and set it aside.

5. Measure around the middle of the flashlight with the tape measure and add 1 inch (2.5 cm) to the measurement. Strip the plastic from one end of the electrical wire down as far as the measurement you just took. Wrap the exposed wires around the middle of the flashlight like fingers so the flashlight doesn't slide out of position (figure 2).

6. Lay the other end of the electrical wire flat against the lazy Susan, over the X mark. With help from an adult, use the drill to make three holes through the wire and into the top of the lazy Susan. Set the screws with the screwdriver through the washers and into the holes in the wire and lazy Susan (figure 3).

7. Drill another hole next to the electrical wire on the lazy Susan. Use the pliers to bend one end of the 12-inch (30.5 cm) piece of coat-hanger wire into a small loop. Hold the loop against the top of the lazy Susan, over the hole, and place a washer on top of it. Twist the last screw through the washer and the wire loop to hold the wire to the lazy Susan (figure 3). Bend or twist the wire, back and forth, to the tip.

8. Make a hole through the center of the small ball with either a drill or hammer and nail. Stick the end of the coat-hanger wire into the hole in the ball. You could also wrap the end of the wire around the ball or use tape to hold it in place.

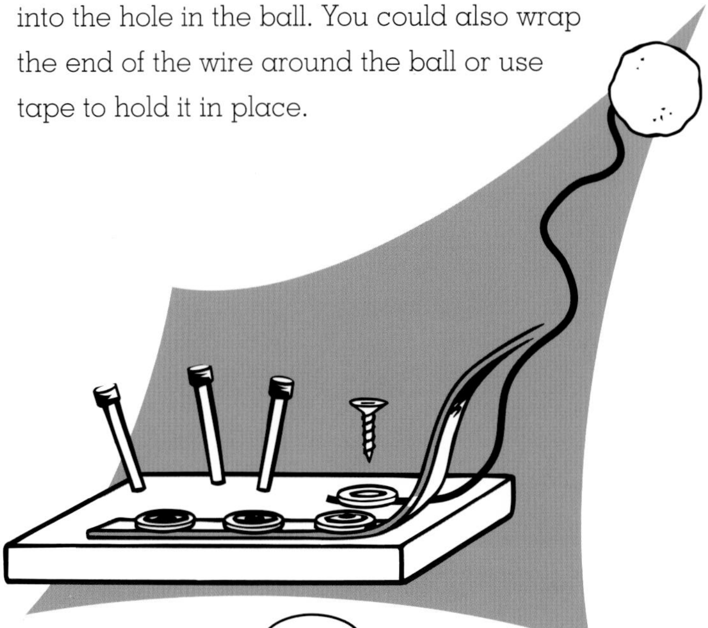

Fig. 1

Fig. 2

Fig. 3

9. Transform the flashlight into a rocket ship by attaching parts of old toys, colored wire, bottlecaps, jar lids, knobs, and other objects to the end and sides of the flashlight with wire, tape, or epoxy. Make sure you don't cover up the lightbulb or the on/off switch.

10. Paint the lazy Susan and set it aside to dry. Use a different color of paint to sign your name on the base.

11. Ten...9...8... Push the bowling ball back in place on the nails...7...6...5...Bend the electrical wire so the rocket ship looks like it's flying...4...3...2...give the lazy Susan a spin...1...Blast off!

IT DOESN'T END HERE

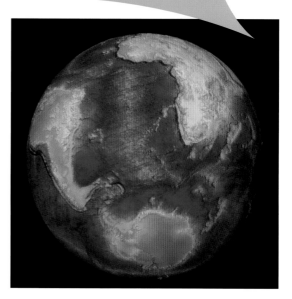

A lot of good has come from the discoveries people have made over the past few thousand years, but some of those inventions and experiments have left us with a big, costly mess to clean up. In this book, we've shown you lots of techniques for creating new things from trash, but the best tool in the world for cleaning up the environment is sitting right there on your shoulders. Use that rounded noggin of yours to learn how things work and how they don't, to come up with new ideas, to listen to other people's opinions, and to share what you learn with your family and friends. In a world of 6 billion people (estimated to reach 9 billion or more by 2050), we all need to work together to find new ways of sharing the space and resources left on our home planet. After all, last time we checked, there wasn't another Earth spinning next door for us to move to. So go forth! Empty those garbage cans, dig through the piles of junk in your garage, and keep tinkering to come up with your own awesome, Earth-friendly inventions. There's a lot of work to do to clean up the planet, and a lot of amazing things still to discover about our Earth.

Templates

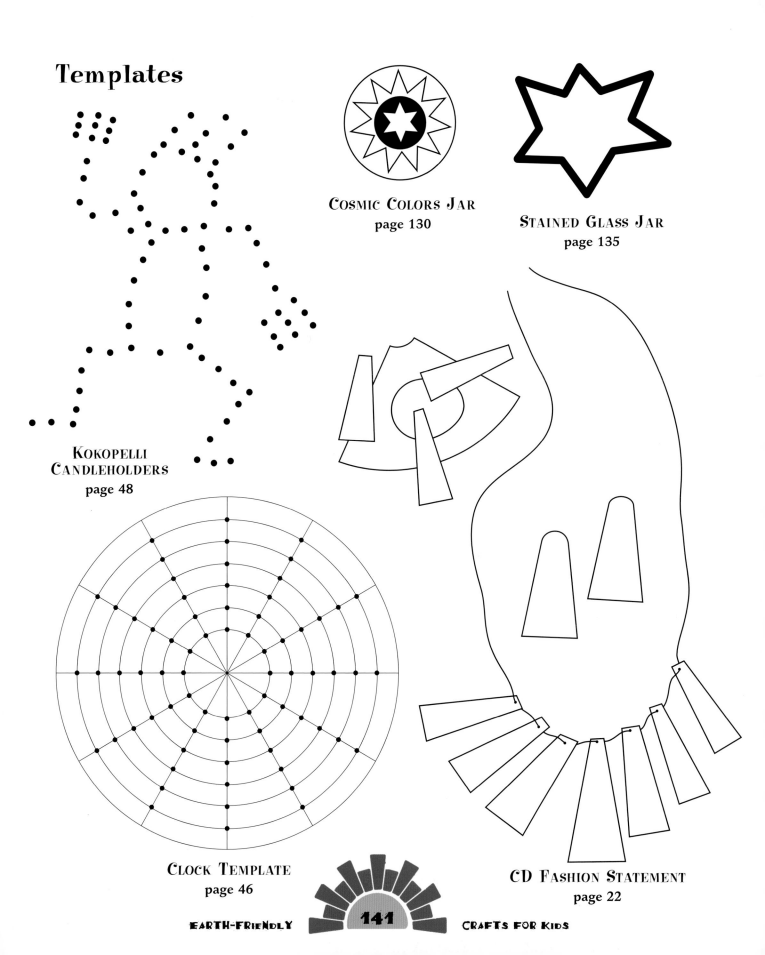

COSMIC COLORS JAR
page 130

STAINED GLASS JAR
page 135

KOKOPELLI CANDLEHOLDERS
page 48

CLOCK TEMPLATE
page 46

CD FASHION STATEMENT
page 22

A Big List of Thanks

The projects in this book evolved from the creative efforts of some big kids at heart:

Lisa Colby (Memory Matchboxes, Picture Perfect Photo Album) manipulates precious metals to produce fine jewelry for stores and galleries throughout the United States. Outside of her studio, she combines her creativity with that of her daughter Celeste and husband Robert.

Jimmy Descant (Spinning Space Sculpture [VFR Pi 2]) has been assembling found objects from thrift stores and garage sales to create one-of-a-kind rocket ships since 1996. You can find more of his space-inspired sculptures at: www.deluxerocketships.com.

Jodi Ford (CD Disco Ball, The "I Can't Believe I Ate Pizza Out of This Box Last Night" Box, Wrinkled Wax Batiks), is a graduate of The Savannah College of Art & Design with a degree in illustration. She is employed by the Asheville Art Museum and works as a freelance designer.

Pamela Granger Gale (CD Fashion Statements, Recycled Bookmarks, Secret Journal, Kokopelli Candleholders, Handmade Paper, Paper Beads) shares her creativity with kids as an art teacher and mother. While able to turn trash into treasure, her true specialty is papermaking.

Deitra Garden (Cap & Lid Curtain Alarm, Flat Tire Picture Frames, Soda Can Bug, Plastic Bag Mat, Stamping with Polystyrene, Newspaper Shelf) is a recognized art educator and freelance designer. She is constantly tinkering with new materials and techniques for artistic expression and creative utility to the benefit (and occasional amusement) of her husband Sean and family of animals: Jake, Ruby, and Junior.

Annie Jacobs (Handy-Dandy Denim Wallet, Scrap Fabric Message Board, Creative Ways to Take Out the Trash) is a freelance gardener and artist who has been sewing since she was 12 years old. When she isn't spending time designing gardens and finding new uses for discarded stuff, she lends her skills and enthusiasm to nonprofit organizations for children and the environment in Asheville, North Carolina.

Billy Jonas (Tin Can Xylophone, Billy Jonas Juguitar) can be heard bangin' and sangin' all over North America and may soon be coming to a school near you. You can see more of his salvaged instruments and listen to his music at www.BILLYJONAS.com or write to Lloyd Artists, 133 Forest Hill Drive, Asheville, NC, USA, 28803.

Diana Light (Fabulous Film Canister Minilights, Flutterby-Butterfly Filters, Pick-up Sticks, For Girls Only—Handy Holder & Picture Frame, Salvaged Seat, Better-Than-a-Broken-Dish Tray, Good-Luck Gift Mirrors, Glass Jar & Bottle Art) is an accomplished artisan who has proven, time-and-again, her ability to turn any object into something cool and useful.

Jeff Menzer (Pocket-People, Sensational Snakes, The...Dinosaur Clock and Album Clock, Luau Snowglobe, Creative Ways to Take Out the Trash) combines his passions for nature and art to demonstrate the potential uses for scrap materials and other people's junk. With his partner Annie Jacobs, Jeff focuses most of his efforts on transforming landscapes with reusable materials.

Lee, Jeffrey and **Eliot Poe** (Recycled Rain Stick) joined their clever heads together to assist the editor with dreaming up projects for this book. As a family, they are always exploring their abilities together, from making household objects to paddling the rivers of North Carolina.

Linda Smith (Super Stylin' Desk Set) can never have too many organizers. When she's through battling for justice in the courtroom, running a restaurant, and helping to sort out other people's lives, she relaxes by crafting, knitting, gardening, and caring for her cats and one cranky bird.

Personal thanks to:

My partner in publication, Joe Rhatigan, for his patience, constant nudging, and much needed sense of humor (you have taught me valuable lessons); Deborah Morgenthal for encouragement, wise advice, and meaningful gestures; Carol Taylor for room to grow and many opportunities at Lark Books; Kathy Holmes for her enthusiasm and creativity (I've truly enjoyed combining our skills to produce this vibrant book); Orrin Lundgren for tidying up my visions with his illustrator's pen; Evan Bracken for capturing the best moments on film; Veronika Gunter and Rain Newcomb for patience, valuable observations, and friendship; Dawn Cusick for listening and advice; the many other folks at Lark Books who lent their trash and their skills; Emmye Taft and Andrew Cahn for encouragement and nourishing food; Linda Smith for proving that persistence and determination will get a person through the thickest of muck; Uncle David, for clearing the air and lifting my spirits; and for most of the above and everything in between, Jake.

Thank you to the wonderful, energetic crew of kids who posed for pictures, tested projects, and gave us their best:

Wesley Albrecht

Naomi Joyce Belz

Drew Timothy Belz

Lauren Hall Christian

Michael Foster

Jesse Louzon-Hadley

Travis Nash

Amber Sherer

Celeste Sherer

Allison Kate Sprague

Morgan Rebecca Sprague

Torre Kieyanna White

Sara Yoeun

and especially

Karla Holmes Weis

&

Jessamyn Britton Weis.

Thanks to the following sources for providing Earth-friendly information:

The Ocean Conservancy for information and photos relating to the International Coastal Cleanup (page 97), 1725 DeSales St., NW, Suite 600, Washington DC, USA, www.oceanconservancy.org

United Nations Environment Program for up-to-date global environmental information at: www.unep.org

United States Geological Service for mining information and the volcano photo (page 44), www.usgs.gov

NASA-Johnson Space Center for the Earth image (cover) and the Orbital Debris Research Project for the photo (page 136) and information about space trash, www.nasa.gov

NAPCOR for PET plastics recycling information and the plastic bottles photo (page 12), www.napcor.com

The United States Environmental Protection Agency www.epa.gov

Conservatree, 100 Second Avenue, San Francisco, CA, USA 94118, www.conservatree.com

PaperU, TAPPI, PO Box 105113, Atlanta, GA 30348-5113, www.tappi.org/paperu

The American Plastics Council, 1300 Wilson Boulevard, Suite 800, Arlington, VA, USA 22209, www.plastics.org

The Global Recycling Network online at http://grn.com

The Aluminum Association, Inc., 900 19th st., NW, Washington, DC, USA, 20006, www.aluminum.org

Photography:
Jim West Photography: trash dump (page 6); plastic recycling (page 13); young organic gardener (page 62); clearcut, old growth forest (pages 72 and 73); tree planters (page 85), glassblower and sand dunes (page 110). Jimwestphoto.com

Bill Morgenstern: paper mill (page 72). Earth Moods Photography, Ontario, Canada, e-mail: emp@ff.lakeheadu.ca

Public Works Department, Asheville, North Carolina, USA: recycling images (page 103)

Corbis: real snake (page 16), aluminum foil (page 57)

United States Fish & Wildlife Service: wildlife (page 62, 73, 97)

Leslie Shaw for providing the Billy Jonas images (page 64)

Heather S. Smith: sheep (page 13), mountains (page 7, 44), ocean (97)

Weststock: girl with compost bin (page 102)

www.comstock.com: detective (page 31)

Index

Absolutely Fabulous, One-of-a-Kind, Dinosaur Griddle Clock, 46-47
aluminum, 57

Bead & Star Bottle, 131
Better-Than-a-Broken Dish Tray, 117-119
Billy Jonas, 64
Billy Jonas Juguitar, 68-70

Candy Tin Travel Games, 58-59
Cap & Lid Curtain Alarm, 26-27
CD Fashion Statement, 22-23
CD Disco Ball, 17-18
cleaning up, 10
composting, 62, 102-103
Cosmic Colors Jar, 130
cutting, 8

Decoupage Bottle, 134
decoupage glue, 9
definitions, 11
dinosaurs, 12

Earth-friendly home, 120-121
Earth-friendly yard, 116
Etched Glass Bottle, 132-133

Fabric scraps, 54-56
Fabulous Film Canister Mini-lights, 35-37
Flutter-By Butterfly Filters, 80-81

Glass Jar & Bottle Art, 129
glass: facts, 118; history and uses, 110-111
Glow-in-the-Dark Mobile, 24-25
glue, 8-9
Good Luck Gift Mirrors, 126-128
Great Paper Bead Resource Page, 80

Handmade Paper & Recycled Envelopes, 74-76

"I Can't Believe I Ate Pizza Out of This Box Last Night" Box, 88-90
International Coastal Cleanup, 97

Kokopelli Candleholders, 48-49

Landfill, 26, 71
Luau Snow Globe, 112-113

Make Your Own Lamp, 60-61
materials and tools, 8-10; and adult assistance, 10; drill and drill bits, 10; glue gun and glue sticks, 9; hammer and nail, 10; tumbler, 10
measuring, 8
Memory Matchboxes, 86-87
metal: facts, 57, 67; history and uses, 44-45
musical instruments, 64-70

Newspaper Shelf, 104-106

Ocean pollution, 97
Odds & Ends 20
Odds & Ends: Flat Tire Picture Frames, 42-43
Odds & Ends: Handy Dandy Denim Wallet, 54-56
Odds & Ends: Handy Holder Picture Frame, 91-93
Odds & Ends: Pocket People, 20-21
Odds & Ends: Scrap Fabric Message Board, 107-109
Odds & Ends: Spinning Space Sculpture, 137-140
Odds & Ends: Wrinkled Wax Batiks, 122-125

Pack an Earth-Friendly Lunch, 19
packaging, 19,
painting, 9-10
paper: facts, 80, 106, 109; history and uses, 72-73
Paper Bead-It, 77-78
Pick-Up Sticks, 82-84
Picture Perfect Photo Album, 94-96
plastic: facts, 26, 31; history and uses, 12-13; identification codes, 31
plastic bags, 26, 28-30, 31
Plastic Scavenger Hunt, 31
Plastic Bag Mat, 28-30

Recycled Rain Stick, 100-101
Recycled Bookmarks, 38-39

Salvaged Seat, 98-99
Secret Journal, 40-41
Sensational Snakes, 14-16
Simple Things You Can Do to Be Earth-Friendly, 62-63
Soda Can Bug, 52-53
space trash, 136
Stained Glass Jar, 135
Stamping with Polystyrene, 32-34
Super Stylin' Desk Set, 50-51

Templates, 141; using them, 8
Terrific Terrariums, 114-115
Tin Can Xylophone, 65-67
trees, 63, 85
tumbler, 10, 117-119

Where Your Trash Ends Up, 71
work space, 8
worms, 103